PENGUIN B
THE VIJAY MALLYA STORY

K. Giriprakash has over twenty years of journalism experience. He has covered a variety of sectors including the liquor industry. He is the chief of bureau and deputy editor at *The Hindu Business Line* in Bangalore, and was previously the chief of bureau of *Business Standard*. He has had stints with Reuters and the *Pioneer* in New Delhi. He lives with his wife and son in Bangalore.

THE Vijay Mallya STORY

K. GIRIPRAKASH

PORTFOLIO
PENGUIN

PORTFOLIO

Published by the Penguin Group

Penguin Books India Pvt. Ltd, 11 Community Centre, Panchsheel Park, New Delhi 110 017, India

Penguin Group (USA) Inc., 375 Hudson Street, New York, New York 10014, USA

Penguin Group (Canada), 90 Eglinton Avenue East, Suite 700, Toronto, Ontario, M4P 2Y3, Canada (a division of Pearson Penguin Canada Inc.)

Penguin Books Ltd, 80 Strand, London WC2R 0RL, England

Penguin Ireland, 25 St Stephen's Green, Dublin 2, Ireland (a division of Penguin Books Ltd)

Penguin Group (Australia), 707 Collins Street, Melbourne, Victoria 3008, Australia (a division of Pearson Australia Group Pty Ltd)

Penguin Group (NZ), 67 Apollo Drive, Rosedale, Auckland 0632, New Zealand (a division of Pearson New Zealand Ltd)

Penguin Books (South Africa) (Pty) Ltd, Block D, Rosebank Office Park, 181 Jan Smuts Avenue, Parktown North, Johannesburg 2193, South Africa

Penguin Books Ltd, Registered Offices: 80 Strand, London WC2R 0RL, England

First published in Portfolio by Penguin Books India 2014

Copyright © K. Giriprakash 2014

All rights reserved

10 9 8 7 6 5 4 3 2 1

ISBN 9780143419013

Typeset in Minion Regular by SÜRYA, New Delhi
Printed at Manipal Technologies Ltd, Manipal

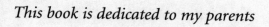

This book is dedicated to my parents

Contents

1

A Magnate in the Making

'Are you all right, Vittal?'

The takeover tycoon lay still. There was panic all around the Taj Hotel in Bombay (now Mumbai). Some of the hotel staffers were running helter-skelter while guests crowded around the inert Vittal Mallya, too stunned to react.

'The party should have gotten over long ago. Just see what happened,' one of the partygoers complained to his friend as they got ready to attend the funeral, reflecting that if the party had ended earlier, Vittal Mallya might have been saved. But as late night parties go, the one on the night of 12 December 1983 had seemed never ending.

The doctors who were summoned to attend to Mallya pronounced him dead. The fifty-eight-year-old tycoon had suffered a massive heart attack, his second, and passed away instantly. The bespectacled man who commanded immediate respect from anyone who met him had been a workaholic; he had not slowed down a bit even as he grew older.

A day after Mallya's death, his embalmed body was brought to the official headquarters of United Breweries at Brewery House on Grant Road in Bangalore (now Bengaluru) for employees, friends and relatives to pay their respects. His son Vijay was in New York, attending to business connected with the international operations of the company when he received the tragic news. Vijay Mallya who was twenty-eight years old at that time, was shattered. His mind and emotions about his late father in turmoil and trying to grapple with the thoughts of what the future held for him, he took the next flight back home. 'I suddenly realized that the buck stops with me,' he said later, thinking back on that journey.

On his return, he was met by his stepmother Ritu. Vittal Mallya had married her after divorcing Vijay's mother, Lalitha. There may have been some uneasiness between father and son, but there was never any public display of animosity between the two.

Vijay quickly got down to the task of preparing for his father's last rites while the corporate sector got busy speculating whether Mallya's son, still very inexperienced, would take over the business empire or if it would be split vertically. Tragedies are usually a time of mourning, but in the case of business families, unfortunately, they are more of an occasion to debate the succession plan.

~

Vittal Mallya was born in Dhaka (now in Bangladesh) on 8 February 1924 to Devi and Dr (Lt Col.) Bantwal Ganapathi Mallya. He was the youngest of three children. It is believed that a young Vijay Mallya wanted to be a doctor like his grandfather but circumstances prevented him from doing so.

Vittal Mallya studied at the prestigious Doon School in Dehradun and later at the Presidency College in Calcutta (now Kolkata) where he had an outstanding academic record. Even though Vittal could have easily got a well-paying job in the corporate sector or anywhere else, he chose to become an entrepreneur. He made a few attempts at starting his own business, and was eventually drawn to the liquor industry after he happened to come across the balance sheet of a liquor company. Adept at analysing balance sheets, Vittal Mallya saw the immense potential for good returns the industry had to offer provided one could run the business in a professional manner. He also realized that he could use the profits generated from this company to diversify into other industries and build lasting assets. Vittal's ambition was to build a huge business conglomerate with diversified interests. In fact, the assets he created during his time helped his son raise resources for his manifold businesses.

The company that immediately caught his attention was United Breweries Ltd which was founded in 1915 and was run by the British. In its earlier avatar, it used to sell bulk beer to British troops in the mid-nineteenth century. Before long, Mallya started acquiring shares of United Breweries and within a couple of years had gathered a substantial stake in the company. If things had remained the same, he would have got good dividends from the company year after year but a stroke of good fortune completely changed his profile. In 1947, when India got independence, most

Britishers who had business interests in the country, started abandoning their companies to return to their homeland. In the case of United Breweries, impressed with Mallya's intelligence, the management handed over the reins of the company to him. So at the age of twenty-two, Vittal Mallya became the head of a large company. And so began his tryst with the liquor industry.

Four years after taking over United Breweries, Mallya made his first acquisition: McDowell and Company Ltd, a company based in Madras (now Chennai). At that time, McDowell was an importer of foreign liquor brands, tea and tobacco products.

In 1959, Mallya set up the company's first distillery in Kerala as part of a backward integration plan. He also struck a deal with the owners of some of the foreign brands to start producing them locally with value addition coming in the form of imported concentrates. Mallya's genius was at play again when he decided to market these Indian substitutes of foreign liquor as 'Indian Made Foreign Liquor' (IMFL)—a term that continues to be used even today by domestic liquor manufacturers.

Mallya was also the first to give the label 'No. 1' to the names of certain liquor products like McDowell's brandy—a now-popular phrase used by liquor makers across the country for some of their products. Mallya expanded his business further by setting up greenfield distilleries in Andhra Pradesh and Goa. He also acquired companies like Carew & Co. which had distilleries in Uttar Pradesh, West Bengal and Bangladesh, and Phipson & Co. in Calcutta, where his son Vijay earned his spurs. When Vijay turned eighteen, he appointed him a director in McDowell and Co.

Vittal Mallya hit pay dirt again when a new government took over the reins of the country after winning the general elections in 1977 by defeating Indira Gandhi's Congress party. Morarji Desai, the new prime minister, whose ideology was based on Gandhian principles, decided to impose prohibition in the country which meant a total ban on the sale of liquor. It left owners of distilleries and breweries in total disarray and out of business. Several of them started selling off their assets at knock-down prices as they believed prohibition would continue for a long time. But Mallya firmly believed that the government would not be able to sustain such a policy interminably as it would lead to a rise in the sale of cheap and spurious liquor. They would have to lift the ban on the sale of liquor sooner than later.

Therefore, he started scouting around for cheap acquisitions and before long he had nine of them in his portfolio, some of which were bought at throwaway prices.

As Mallya anticipated, prohibition was eventually lifted. Desai's government was defeated at the hustings two years later and Indira Gandhi returned to power. By the time she rolled back the policy, Mallya had acquired most of the liquor companies on sale. The only big competitors United Breweries had at that time were Mohan Meakin in the north, which had the distinction of setting up Asia's first brewery in India, and Shaw Wallace in the east. While Mohan Meakin was gradually edged out of the market over time, Shaw Wallace was eventually acquired by Mallya's son.

Vittal's successes began to be noticed by the corporate sector. Along with textile czar Dhirubhai Ambani, who was making a mark at the time in Bombay, Mallya became the toast of the corporate world. A magazine even gave him the moniker 'Takeover Tycoon'. But Mallya was not content with expanding his brewery and distillery businesses. He had a vision to create diversified empire with companies ranging from liquor to food to pharmaceuticals. To give impetus to his ambitions, he began acquiring shares in the chocolate behemoth Cadbury; Kissan, which makes jams and ketchups; and Herbertsons, which manufactured Dipy's jelly crystals, a popular product those days. The Kerala-based Dalco Cannings, which made pickles and mango products, was another company he added to his already bulging portfolio of acquisitions. He also bought a stake in pharma majors, Hoechst (now Sanofi), Russell Pharma, the eyecare company Optrix, which had a manufacturing plant in Srinagar in Jammu and Kashmir, and Hindustan Polymers.

In a short period of time, Vittal Mallya had expanded his business empire fast and wide. But behind these acquisitions was not only a man with great vision but also someone who was extremely careful with money. Mallya used to review every invoice on a daily basis, checking each and every figure in it. If there was a discrepancy of even one paisa he would instantly instruct one of his secretaries (and there were three of them: Lobo, Govindan and K. Rao) to immediately take up the matter with the official concerned.

U.B. Bhat, who worked closely with both father and son, recalls that while some considered Vittal Mallya stingy, his employees and stakeholders admired him for being thrifty. Bhat says that everyone in the company understood that any wastage would not be taken to very kindly by the management. 'It sent the message that when the chairman could be so careful about money, everyone down the line should be careful about it as well.'

On one occasion, a manager who had accompanied Mallya to Bombay saw him spending several minutes examining a bill after checking out of the five-star Taj Mahal Hotel and punching some numbers into his watch which had an inbuilt calculator. This happened again when both of them checked out of another five-star hotel in Panaji in Goa some time later. The manager was extremely puzzled. On the way back to the airport, he mustered up enough courage to ask his boss why he was checking every bill. 'Sir, do you think a five-star hotel would cheat us?' he asked. Mallya replied that the money he was spending belonged to the shareholders and as he was the custodian of their company, he had to be doubly careful while using their resources.

Along with being an astute businessman, Vittal Mallya was considered a fair and just boss. Bhat, who graduated from IIM, Ahmedabad, joined United Breweries in 1978 after being personally interviewed by Mallya. Bhat's appointment letter said that he was entitled to an office car from the day he joined duty. However, on his first day at work, Bhat was informed that his car, an Ambassador, would be delivered only in a week's time.

Cars were considered a luxury item even as late as the 1990s in corporate India. It took months for delivery as government policies did not allow private sector companies such as Hindustan Motors, which manufactured Ambassadors in its plant in West Bengal, to expand their capacity despite the rise in demand.

At the end of Bhat's first day at work, he was about to hitch a ride home with his friend when Vittal Mallya called. 'Hope you have the car to go home,' said Mallya. On learning that Bhat had been asked to wait at least a week for the car to be delivered to him, Mallya immediately instructed his secretary to place his own car—a Standard Herald—at Bhat's disposal until the Ambassador was delivered.

The company had promised him a car on the day he joined; a promise once made had to be kept.

'With such a person as your boss, you will give hundred per cent to the company,' Bhat later told one of his colleagues.

No employee, even those who came on board after an acquisition, ever went without a salary no matter how bad the situation in some of the companies was. Mallya never refused an invitation from his managers to visit their homes during social occasions even though he was known to be publicity shy and reticent. 'He was a completely different person when he used to visit us at home. He would crack jokes, enjoy himself and even send instructions before reaching their homes on how he would like his wine to be served,' recalls an old colleague.

An extremely scrupulous man, Vittal Mallya was always known to work within the boundaries of the law. If he went abroad and didn't spend all the foreign exchange he was allotted by the government, he would remit the remaining amount to the government immediately upon his return. Never one to stand on false prestige, he carried postal mails meant for overseas distributors along with him whenever he travelled. He would then invite the distributor to his hotel and personally hand over the mail to him.

Vittal Mallya ran his businesses with a nearly non-existent hierarchy; what is now commonly known as a flat organization. Most of the senior managers reported directly to Mallya or to M. Srinivas Rao, his confidant, who headed both the brewery and distillery divisions.

But when the young Vijay Mallya started involving himself closely with the group, his father put in another layer between himself and the rest, asking all the senior managers to report to Rao and Vijay.

Once Vijay Mallya took over the reins, the structure was changed completely—Vijay brought in a corporate management structure professionalizing the organization in keeping with the new economic order. Each division had a president, a vice president and managers who had clearly defined roles.

~

Vijay was born to Lalitha Ramaiah and Vittal Mallya on 18 December 1955 in Calcutta where his parents had settled down. He studied at the prestigious La Martiniere School and later graduated in commerce from St Xavier's. The experiences he had during his years at La Martiniere largely defined Mallya.

'Whatever I am today is because of the exposure I had in school with regard to extra curricular activities. It helped me to go out and face the world,' Mallya admitted in his speech at the school's 176th Founder's Day celebrations in 2011.

According to one of his classmates, everyone in the school, including the teachers and the principal knew that Vijay was the son of business tycoon Vittal Mallya. Potential troublemakers and bullies kept a safe distance from him but his teachers remained unaffected by his pedigree and did not hesitate in disciplining him whenever it was needed

Mallya was quite proud of his school's club, the Hastings Club, which he later represented as its captain. His affinity for everything red comes from the red-coloured flag of the club. Anil Mukherjee, his senior in school, has been quoted recounting how he pulled up Vijay once for maintaining long hair and sent him home, instructing him to return with cropped hair. At the end of his tenure as captain of the club, Mukherjee passed on the baton to the young Mallya.

Apart from his interest in sports, Mallya participated in several competitions organized in his school and won a few medals as well. For the most part, he was an above average student who never topped his class until a pep talk from his father changed his attitude towards academics.

Vittal Mallya, who had been a brilliant student himself in school, could not tolerate the easy-going attitude of his son. He decided to have a heart-to-heart talk with his son on what he expected from him. He made it clear to him that if he had to make a mark in his life, then he had to lay a foundation for it in school. Plagued by doubt—how could he score more than those who were so good in subjects he was afraid of—Vijay protested to his mother, ranted even, but there was no respite. Mallya decided to give himself a chance and started working hard. He immediately began to see an improvement in his performance and very soon he started topping his class and ended up obtaining a first in the senior level Cambridge exams in the entire state.

Mallya has on several occasions acknowledged the role played by his schoolteachers in turning him into an achiever. In his speech at the 176th anniversary celebration at La Martiniere, Mallya pointed out that his ability to think outside the box and his superior communication skills are a result of the training he received in his school. 'If you can communicate well, half the battle is won. It is a clear advantage over others. Many jobs have been abandoned halfway through because the people didn't have confidence in themselves.'

There were other qualities for which Mallya was famous in his school. He used to have the silencer removed from his Standard Herald car whenever he took it to school, creating a huge din that caught everyone's attention instantly. Such attention-seeking later gave way to Mallya donning a larger-than-life persona in his professional career. Anything Mallya does is backed by enormous publicity, resulting in big coverage in the media. He once told a journalist that he himself is his brand's biggest ambassador.

After Vijay graduated in commerce from St Xavier's, his father decided that he should start learning the ropes of the business—a clear sign that he expected Vijay to take over once he retired. Vijay started working under of one of Vittal's most trusted lieutenants, H.P. Bhagat, who headed the group's Calcutta-based Phipson & Co., a distributor of beer and liquor, including the popular Black Dog whisky, Kalyani Black Label and Sun Lager beer.

Bhagat, an IIT graduate, was considered a giant

in the liquor industry. Vijay couldn't have found a better mentor than him. Although Vijay was the heir apparent, Bhagat did not hesitate to put him through the paces. As part of his training Vijay was asked to visit liquor shops across West Bengal to get a grasp of how products were retailed at the ground level. He would spend the entire day at the shops interacting with customers as well as vendors, absorbing the experience. There were occasions when he would travel by bicycle to reach places which did not have motorable roads. Such intense training gave Mallya a strong foundation in the liquor industry. If he is held in awe by his peers in the industry across the world, it is because of his sound understanding of the intricacies of the liquor business.

The liquor trade in India is heavily dependent on the whims and fancies of the local state government. At one extreme, the state may decide to ban liquor sales altogether. On the other, it might allow the unhindered sale of liquor by manipulating licences and granting them to only certain sections of society, existing licence holders or those who fund political parties. However, prohibition as a policy has never worked successfully. Gujarat, the birthplace of

Mahatma Gandhi, has imposed total prohibition on liquor sales for decades. But it is a well-known fact that the ban has not been very effective and liquor continues to be freely available in the black market. And worse, the state continues to lose out on excise duties and other tax revenues it could earn from the authorized sale of liquor.

In Karnataka, the home state of the Mallyas and the Khodays, successive governments have discreetly promoted the liquor industry over the years. Bangalore, the state capital, is home to the largest number of pubs in the country and during the 1980s, the single biggest attraction for a tourist visiting the city were the numerous pubs sporting names such as Nasa, and Night Watchman. In neighbouring Tamil Nadu, however, the laws are as stiff as they come: one cannot sell liquor products made in another state; they have to be produced locally to be sold there.

Most states in the country also impose an entry tax on liquor brands produced outside the state. If a liquor manufacturer wants to sell his brands outside his own state, he has to pay a tax for that as well. Thus, any liquor being transported across state lines is taxed both ways. Liquor makers, unlike other

FMCG companies, cannot set prices on their own. The respective state governments decide what the price of each bottle should be, sometimes taking years to revise the prices. As the liquor business normally involves huge margins, at times as much as 40 per cent, manufacturers are able to sail through periods during which the prices remain stagnant. Such situations sometimes give way to the possibility of corruption—palms have to be greased to get a price increase. In Andhra Pradesh, which is one of the largest consumers of beer—the other two being Tamil Nadu and Karnataka—the laws are slightly different. The state government buys beer from the manufacturers on the basis of their market share either in the state or nationally: assuming a certain company has a market share of 30 per cent in Andhra Pradesh, the state will buy only that much from it. In certain years, the criteria are changed, and the state government will buy beer based on the national market share of a particular company. The multitude of taxes as well as stiff penalties imposed on liquor companies have resulted in the introduction of some unhealthy practices by some of the players. For example, the practice of using the same licence to manufacture more cases than permitted was prevalent in Karnataka for a long time until it was banned in the early 1990s. Such a practice used to be called 'seconds sale'. This is how it would work: if a liquor company had a licence to manufacture 100 cases per month, it would use the same licence repeatedly to manufacture more cases. As this was unaccounted for, the liquor company would bribe government officials as well as ministers to ensure that it was not penalized for indulging in such unfair practices.

A year or two after Vijay joined Phipson, his father sent him to the US to work with the pharmaceutical giant Hoechst to expose his son to international business practices. Later, Vijay Mallya implemented some of these practices learnt at Hoechst in his own group of companies when he took over the reins.

The stint with Hoechst also shaped Mallya's global ambitions. He kicked off the international operations of the group by starting an international trading arm of Herbertsons in 1978. The company already had a licence to import several products. Therefore, Mallya started importing those which were in short supply in the country, like chemicals, soda ash and even cement. Realizing that his son was showing good business acumen, Vittal Mallya gave him more responsibilities, even asking him to monitor the performance of the senior managers in the group companies.

~

An extraordinary general meeting (EGM) hardly attracts the kind of crowd one finds at an annual general meeting (AGM). But this meeting, called in October 1983, was different. It was called to elect the new chairman of United Breweries.

But much before the EGM, a group of people who were close to Vittal Mallya had held an informal meeting at the residences of one of the distributors of United Breweries. It is not known whether Srinivas Rao and H.P. Bhagat were part of this meeting, but these two certainly were the alternative choices to head the company.

The meeting seemed more like a party but those assembled there had an important agenda to discuss. The group was small, mainly consisting of some of United Breweries' distributors and the company's regional satraps, as Vijay Mallya would call them later. The group also included some of Vittal Mallya's trusted lieutenants. Since Vittal Mallya had not publicly declared his son as his successor, though he was being trained to take over from him eventually, the so-called regional heads of the company thought it fit to assume that their chances of heading the company were as good as anybody's.

The discussion at that secret meeting centered on the likely successor to Vittal Mallya. During the interaction, a couple of names were shortlisted to be proposed during the EGM. But these two never stood a chance once the EGM began.

As the day's business was called to attention, everyone was asked to stand for a minute to condole the demise of the chairman, Vittal Mallya. Then came the crucial moment which would chart the future course of the company. There were about 3000 shareholders assembled at the EGM. When the meeting was called to attention to propose the name of the new chairman, several hands went up in favour of the junior Mallya.

The 'rebel' group was too stunned to react. A few feeble attempts to propose the name of one of the contenders were lost in the commotion.

'It was something that I least expected,' Vijay Mallya was to say later. Most of the shareholders, including those who owed their allegiance to the elder Mallya, didn't want an outsider to be made the chairman. There were others who thought that handing over the reins to the junior Mallya for a couple of years was not a bad idea. If he was not found good enough, he could always be removed.

The fact that the promoter family owned a majority stake in the company, with Vijay Mallya holding two-thirds of the stake in the holding company, Mallya Pvt. Ltd (which has since been merged with UB Holdings), also helped swing the chairmanship Mallya's way.

Thus Vijay Mallya became the new chairman of the company, a position that brought with it enormous wealth and immense responsibility.

In some ways, Mallya realized that getting elected as the chairman of a business empire was far easier compared to running it. While he had worked with international companies such as Hoechst and even as a salesperson cycling from one brewery to another to acquire first-hand knowledge of the Indian market, he had realized the kind of responsibility he was confronted with. 'I had nobody to turn to. I had no choice but to either swim or sink,' Mallya told a gathering of IIT undergrads years later. He, of course, had lieutenants: the four senior managers who headed each region of his company. The only problem was that they had also been contenders for the top post. If he had sought their advice, he would have shown his inadequacies in handling his responsibilities. There was also the fear that they might not give him the right advice.

United Breweries at that stage had a total revenue of about Rs 40 crore and a volume sale of about 3.8 million cases (each case consisting of nine 750 ml bottles).

One of the things Mallya realized was that he had to quickly establish himself in the liquor industry. Unfortunately, he did not have a very successful track record to fall back upon. When he was drafted to work with Carew Phipson soon after he completed his graduation, he was given the task of rebranding the company as well as launching new brands. Carew Phipson's business was skewed towards gin, with 95 per cent sales coming from it. Being a seasonal drink, it did not give year-round sales for the company. Mallya's mandate, therefore, was to create new non-gin brands. It was the first time the twenty-something Mallya had been put in charge of creating new brands. The two brands which he created at that time were Royal Reserve and Splendour. Mid-level managers were instructed in no uncertain terms that these were the projects of the boss's son and so they had better put in their best effort to promote the brands. Mallya earmarked huge amounts of money for the advertising and marketing expenses for promoting these brands. Very unlike his father who believed in letting the brands fend for themselves.

Vijay Mallya once claimed that for him brands are like animals; they are not inanimate objects and hence it is important to constantly reinforce the ties that bind the brand with the consumer.

In spite of his best efforts, the two brands he created, bombed in the market. As the marketing and promotional activities had entailed a lot of expenditure, he was seen as someone who had squandered the company's money for brands which did not produce commensurate sales. The debacle weighed heavily on Vijay because some of Vittal Mallya's close associates held it against him claiming that he was not competent enough to become the chairman of the company.

Contenders like H.P. Bhagat and Vittal's right-hand man, M. Srinivas Rao, were considered better candidates. In fact, Rao, with his impeccable record of turning around sick companies and growing non-liquor businesses, was the front runner for the chairmanship. Even the Mallya family had felt that the business should be presided over by one of Vittal Mallya's close associates until such time as Vijay was ready to take over the reins. There was also the fear that, given his record, Vijay might squander away all the wealth. Critics cited several instances of his weakness for glitz and glamour, particularly his penchant for flying in hordes of his friends, and sometimes his dogs as well, when he travelled from Calcutta to Bangalore. The expensive makeover he ordered for the Herbertsons' office in Bombay was another example of Mallya's lavish spending. The office was in the Fort area where most of the buildings are either crumbling structures or have Victorian designs. Mallya decided to give it a new look and had one of the floors done up with smoked glass and granites. When he invited his father to inaugurate the newly designed office floor, the first thing Vittal Mallya said after cutting the ribbon and within everyone's earshot was, 'How easy it is to spend money.'

But all that was in the past. Vijay Mallya had a big job at hand. His ambition was to turn the company into a billion-dollar enterprise with businesses across several continents. He wanted to usher in a new era quickly and hence decided to induct professionals from across several industries, something other players in the industry had never done before. He also created a think tank-like entity called the central planning and control department (CPCD) which was housed in the headquarters of United Breweries, Brewery House, the hexagonal building at the tail end of Grant Road (now Vittal Mallya Road). Today, these buildings have given way to a shopping mall, office complexes and the JW Marriott Hotel. (Part of the UB City complex is now up for sale to raise money for Mallya to pay off some of his debts.)

Vijay Mallya started hiring executives with consulting and management backgrounds. Some of those recruited at that time were among the best brains in the country—Naaz Roshan, Deepak Anand, Naresh Malhotra, Yogesh Desai and Alok Chandra as well as Sunil Mehra, Biren Ghosh and Ravi Jain, former classmates at his alma mater, St Xavier's.

The message to the board as well as those who had been hired by his father was that while he was professionalizing the company, he was also getting his own people.

It created a situation where the old-timers and associates of Vittal Mallya were sooner or later confined to board positions. The role of the CPCD was simple: to keep a watch on the day-to-day affairs of the company, come up with new strategies to grow the brands and plug loopholes, if any, immediately. Every month, all the members of the CPCD were called for a meeting and asked to make a presentation on the operations of the preceding month. Such exercises helped Mallya stay in touch with all divisions of his company on a regular basis.

Mallya also started overhauling the company's management. In one such rejig, he shifted the head of Punjab Breweries to take over the operations of the entire breweries division, thereby sidelining one of his father's trusted colleagues.

Those failed brands—Royal Reserve and Splendour—were in fact the stepping stones to huge successes for United Breweries and Mallya later.

Vijay Mallya deserves credit for the revival of Kingfisher beer. Today, it is the leading beer brand in the country with a market share of about 50 per cent. There is an interesting tale to the launch of Kingfisher beer and its resurgence. Mohan Meakins' Golden Eagle was the leading brand in the beer segment when Vittal Mallya and Srinivas Rao decided to launch a brand which could take on the competition. While scouting around, they found that one of their top officials had a letter pad with the logo of a kingfisher bird on it. They persuaded the executive to part with the logo, and so the Kingfisher brand was born. Over time, the logo has evolved from depicting a sitting kingfisher to one in mid-flight.

The brand went into hibernation for sometime until Vijay Mallya decided to revive it. He is believed to have conducted his own survey by standing near the gates of several colleges interviewing students on what they thought would work for a brand. The survey yielded some interesting facts: youngsters aspire for brands which enhance their lifestyle as well as those they can connect with. Within months, Kingfisher beer was relaunched and marketed in several parts of the company. However, the biggest problem the brand faced was that it was not pan-Indian. Its distribution network was restricted and as beer is a seasonal drink, its sales in the north were muted.

During those days, the breweries of United Breweries in north India were shut down because of poor sales in the winter months and in the south, where Kingfisher was popular, it was in short supply because the breweries did not have the capacity to cater to the increased demand. The company decided to rationalize production: those breweries which were shut down during the off season in a particular region would be used to manufacture beer and supply to those states where there was a shortfall.

Another issue United Breweries encountered in its retail business was regarding packaging, especially bottles, a key raw material for any liquor company. The packaging costs for a liquor company are huge and if they are not controlled well, they can shave off a large portion of its profits. In the case of United Breweries, even though the invoice included the cost of the bottles, the dealers would either forget to return them or return broken bottles. Therefore, United Breweries had to constantly produce new bottles, which involved a large expenditure.

To arrest this trend, the company management decided to impose a new rule for dealers: they would get a fresh supply of beer cases only when they returned an equal number of bottles. The local 'kabadiwallas' or those who trade in used bottles, play a crucial role in the liquor trade. They are the ones who collect used bottles from those who retail as well as those who consume liquor. In turn, the liquor distributors or dealers buy the used bottles from these kabadiwallas and return them to the manufacturers, thus completing the cycle.

The cycle is broken if the distributors fail to buy bottles from the retail traders, and that was what was happening in the case of United Breweries. But once the new rule was imposed strictly, the company started benefitting from it.

Several years later, the same issue cropped up in a different manner. The traders of used bottles started forming a cartel to extract more money from the distributors, which again hit the manufacturers hard. Therefore, manufacturers started patenting the design of the bottle apart from printing the name of the brand or that of the company on these bottles. Obviously, the traders were forced to sell the bottles only to those companies whose name was printed on them.

In addition to these measures, the price of Kingfisher beer was made uniform so that the landed cost of the beer to the dealer would be the same everywhere irrespective of where it was sourced from.

This exercise was begun in 1984 and by the late 1980s, most of UB Group's breweries had turned profitable.

By early 1986, Golden Eagle had started yielding ground to Kingfisher. By March the same year, Kingfisher was officially declared the largest-selling beer brand in the country.

There were still pockets of the market where Kingfisher beer was still way behind the competing brands. One such market was Bombay. During the late 1980s, Associated Breweries' London Pilsner was the biggest brand in the city, so much so that five-star hotels didn't even bother to offer other brands to their customers.

Once, during his stay at the Taj Mahal hotel, Vijay Mallya happened to order a bottle of Kingfisher beer but was politely informed that the only beer available there was London Pilsner. Not being someone who took no for an answer, he is believed to have summoned one of his top marketing executives to fly down to Bombay to ensure that the Taj started serving Kingfisher as well.

The executive immediately took the next flight to Bombay and sought a meeting with the food and beverage manager, Camellia Punjabi. After some intense negotiations, the hotel agreed to start offering Kingfisher beer to its guests. In turn, United Breweries offered to fund the cost of printing of the hotel's menu cards. Ironically, London Pilsner now is at the same position Kingfisher was in before it entered the Taj, having dropped to an insignificant market share. (United Breweries later went on to acquire Associated Breweries, the makers of London Pilsner.)

While United Breweries kept increasing its market share as well as expanding its portfolio of brands, it failed to recognize the potential of strong beer in the country. The initial hesitancy cost the company several crores as well as leadership in that segment. Some of the top executives did make the company aware of the opportunity strong beer offered but either ego issues or the inability to keep pace with emerging trends made the management completely ignore the suggestions.

According to one of the insiders, a top executive in the company made a strong pitch for launching a strong beer in the market at one of the company's meeting held in Kathmandu in Nepal, but his suggestion was rejected as the management felt that it was ahead of its time and would fail. After all, the idea behind drinking beer was not to get drunk, and there was a chance that any change in its alcohol content might turn out to be counter-productive.

But the executive felt that since various state

governments in India do not have separate tax structures for beer and spirits, consumers were likely to prefer liquor with higher alcohol content at similar prices.

Some of the domestic liquor companies were able to see the potential strong beer had to offer long before United Breweries realized it and launched brands with higher alcohol content. Brands like Haywards 5000, Thunderbolt and Bullet, which had 8 per cent v/v alcohol content (compared with about 5 per cent v/v for normal beer), were launched with great success in the market.

Meanwhile, Mallya started acquiring companies unrelated to his core liquor business—such as Mangalore Chemicals & Fertiliser (MCF) and Best & Crompton Engineering—while exiting those his father had bought like UB Mec, a battery venture, and Kissan. His only major success amidst the mountain of failed acquisitions was Berger Paints. His venture into soft drinks started off with a bang with brands like Rush, Thrill and Sprint that were supposed to take on the multinationals, but these went bust after a short time, forcing the group to write off about Rs 33 crore in losses, a huge amount of money in those days.

But in the breweries business, Mallya confidently strode ahead. While Vittal's legacy to his son was supply-led solidity which meant that the company could supply as well as distribute better than any other company could, what Vijay Mallya brought to the table was his ability to convert supply-led dominance to demand-led dominance.

Mallya has always maintained and zealously promoted the idea that the consumption of liquor is part of one's lifestyle. Therefore, he regularly hired movie actors to promote his brands through surrogate advertising. Some of those who were in charge of such promotions say that several crores were spent in advertising and, initially, even they didn't know what the outcome of such expenditure would be. For example, several lakhs would be spent in sponsoring the derby in Bombay, even though there was no direct connection between the sport and the liquor business. But Mallya always backed such investments in brand building, saying that in the long term this approach would pay off, and ultimately it did.

One of the biggest assets Mallya created to promote his brands was the Kingfisher swimsuit calendar. The limited edition calendar is much sought after by the who's who in the fashion world. It was launched in 2003 and features various models in swimsuits who are photographed on the beaches of Goa, the French Riviera and other such exotic destinations. Ace photographer Atul Kasbekar is involved with the production of the calendar. Those selected to feature in the calendar are seen to receive a huge boost to their careers. Actors Deepika Padukone and Katrina Kaif modelled for the calendar before they were launched in movies.

Mallya is also associated with Formula 1 racing and has his own team. This again is one of the properties which he has used effectively to promote his brands. Mallya's interest in racing can be attributed to his childhood fantasy of owning a Ferrari. He did have one when he was just four years old. But that one was a toy car, gifted to him by his father.

His overriding passion for cars drew him to India's only racing track at that time in Sholavaram, near Madras. Between the 1960s and the late 1980s, it was the hub of motor racing in India. Since then the action has shifted to Irrangatukottai, further away from the city, and then on to the Formula 1 racing track in Noida, near New Delhi.

When Mallya was still in his twenties, he decided to participate in motor racing events. He enrolled himself with the Madras motor racing club and started training for one of the races in Sholavaram. But his debut season was a disaster. He lost his first race to the Maharajakumar of Gondal. The Gondal king's car was not only better suited for racing conditions but had a robust engine as well. The Sholavaram track itself was an unused T-shaped air strip left over from the Second World War that had been readied for motor racing by enthusiasts. One could drive between four and six laps on it. Some of the popular motorists included Sundar Karivardhan and Vicky Chandok who later became a friend of Mallya. Chandok is now the president of the Federation of Motor Sports Clubs of India. He, with some generous financial assistance from Mallya, brought the Formula 1 world championships to India. Mallya also co-owns a Formula 1 team, Force India, with businessman Subroto Ray's Sahara India Parivar. A few years ago, the Lucknow-based company bought a 42.5 per cent stake in Force India for an estimated $100 million and the racing team is now known as Sahara Force India. Mallya and the Mol family from the Netherlands had earlier bought the

Silverstone-based Formula 1 team from Spyker for about 88 million euros in 2007. Force India's car VJM-01 is named after Mallya and the Mol family members, Jan and Michiel.

Sahara Force India hasn't had a good run so far. In 2012, the team was placed ninth in the world championship with a score of 13 points. To add to its misfortune, its co-owner, Sahara India, has recently fallen foul of the Indian regulator, the Securities and Exchange Board of India (SEBI), for violating public issue norms. The Supreme Court recently barred its promoter Subrata Roy from leaving the country and selling off its properties.

Coming back to the racing at Sholavaram: Mallya eventually did win against the Maharajakumar of Gondal on the strength of the superior quality of his car's engine. 'The loss sort of made Mallya buy a better racing car,' one of his close associates said later.

For Mallya, the two businesses of breweries and distilleries and his personality were inherently suited; each was an extension of the other. Almost everyone associated with him says that Mallya is perhaps one of the brightest people they have ever met—a man who knows his numbers well, works hard and plays hard in equal measure. He never keeps a file pending beyond a day. He is also known to have a near photographic memory and the gift of the gab.

While he never micromanaged his various businesses, he was seen by his critics as someone who had started surrounding himself with those who told him what he liked to hear.

One of the reasons he chose to get himself NRI status was so he would be able to make international forays. NRIs are allowed to acquire immovable properties abroad from earnings made in foreign shores. Their earnings from abroad are also exempt from several taxes in the country.

The acquisition of Berger Paints after he became an NRI was not without drama. It was also perhaps one of the few occasions when he made money hand over fist in a business unrelated to liquor.

Berger Paints was owned by different promoters in different parts of the world. It was put up for sale in several countries. Mallya decided to bid for one of the regions and directed one of his top executives to negotiate with the promoters. The deal was finally stuck at £15 million and the executive went back to Mallya informing him that the funds had to be arranged quickly to acquire the company. To which Mallya is believed to have said that the executive's job was not complete yet—he had to arrange for the money as well. The executive managed to raise a loan from HSBC Bank after working his contacts there. The bank seemed to be in an obliging mood and even extended an additional loan for settling the legal fees. Berger Paints did not remain in Mallya's portfolio for long. It was eventually sold in 1996 for a profit of $66 million. A very happy Mallya is believed to have rung up his mother after selling the company and boasted that nobody could question him now if he bought a yacht or an aircraft.

However, Mallya had to face failure in the case of the Chennai-based, dead-as-a-duck Best & Crompton Engineering, a manufacturer of industrial pumps and castings for industrial and automotive applications, which he bought in 1989. To raise funds for acquiring the company, United Breweries again had to take up the debt route. This deal was carried out even though several of his colleagues warned him that it wasn't a wise acquisition.

'I told him that everything in this company was fudged. How can you take over a company when you have not completed due diligence? It is going to be an uphill task to revive it. They are showing profits when they have incurred losses and to make matters worse you are paying taxes on that,' a former colleague, who was involved with the deal, said.

Years later, Mallya confessed that he had committed a mistake. He couldn't make the deal work because of the poor culture at the company. Best & Crompton Engineering was later sold off to the Indonesian Polysindo Group in 1998.

Mallya always looked forward to having a luxurious lifestyle. For example, whenever he visited London, he would prefer staying at the iconic Grosvenor Hotel in the tony Mayfair area in London, which used to be the residence of the former dukes of Westminster.

> *A former executive narrates an incident which shows his preference for the good things in life. On one occasion, Mallya had come down to London to visit the Berger Paints' office in London. It was a busy weekday in London. A finance manager—an Englishman—came hurrying into his functional head's office: 'How many cars do you think VJM has?' he popped the question as soon as he entered his boss's room.*
>
> *'Maybe a hundred. Why?'*
>
> *'In our own parking bay, there are enough already. In fact, there are two new Mercedes Benz cars which are standing there right now.'*

'So? Why are you telling me all this?'

'Because VJM wants another Mercedes and he wants it today.'

'So, get him the car.'

'What? Should we waste money on buying a car which we already have several of? We need the money for other things. I will go and talk to him,' the Englishman responded.

'I have known VJM for years now. If he wants something, you better get it for him.'

But the Englishman ignored his functional head's advice and went into Vijay Mallya's room to talk him out of buying another car.

An hour later, the functional head received a call from VJM asking him to meet him. He spoke to him in Hindi and, loosely translated, it went something like this: 'Tell this English gentleman I want two Mercedes cars, not one. And if I don't find them parked in my office by evening, then he knows what he needs to do the next day.'

By evening, the two new cars were parked outside the office and the Englishman had successfully evaded a showdown with his boss.

One must admit there were those in his company who did stand up to him and it was assumed that they had fallen foul of him. But to his credit, Mallya never asked them to leave.

Although Vijay Mallya is widely considered flamboyant, he has been known on occasion to show a completely different side to his personality, a generosity of spirit reminiscent of his father. During one of his business trips to Zurich, he took one of his executives who was travelling with him to visit a retail store of Patek Philipe SA, the makers of luxury watches, where he bought a watch worth a cool Rs 2 lakh. (At today's price, the watch would probably be worth Rs 50 lakhs.) But what floored the executive was Mallya's generous offer to buy him a similar watch. An offer that the executive politely refused.

When he was in charge of the international operations of Herbertsons, Mallya came in contact with Rajan Pillai, an ambitious businessman whose personality matched his: both men wanted to make it big in life, were extremely ambitious, led life to the fullest, partied hard and had a fetish for displaying their wealth.

Rajan Pillai was the son of Janardhan Pillai, a cashewnut trader in Kerala. (At the time, Mallya's company got cashewnuts processed in one of Pillais' factories.) A clean-shaven and thickset man, Rajan always gave the impression that he was on his way to conquer every boardroom in Asia. One of the first steps he took in order to fulfil his ambition was to shift base from Kerala. He realized that staying in his home state would not help him achieve his dreams of becoming a major industrialist. Hence he set up his offices in Singapore. Vijay Mallya also set up the head office of his international division in Singapore where cashew kernels were processed before being exported to several countries. He forayed into Australia where he bought cashew farms, and was itching to make a statement with his newly gotten wealth.

On one occasion, Pillai made a splash in London newspapers when he got a private space for himself in Wimbledon which brought him instant recognition as well as fame.

As part of his expansion strategy, Pillai joined hands with the head of the US-based RJR Nabisco, Ross Johnson—a move which proved to be his undoing. RJR Nabisco was a tobacco and food products company based out of New York, and with the help of Johnson, Rajan floated a company called Britannia Industries Pvt. Ltd (BIPL) through which he controlled a web of companies, including Britannia Industries in India. According to a report in *India Today*, Johnson filed a petition in Singapore after Pillai failed to honour an agreement to repay a loan he had taken from him. The Singapore court charged Pillai with misappropriating BIPL's money and using it to square off transactions of some of his offshore companies. The court also ruled that the entire control of BIPL be taken away from Pillai.

Pillai had also floated a joint venture, Britannia Brands (Holdings) Pvt. Ltd, along with the French food giant Groupe BSN, for controlling operations in India, Pakistan and a few other countries in Asia. But the partners had a falling out after Pillai rejected Groupe BSN's offer to buy out his stake in Britannia. Groupe BSN sued Pillai, stating that he had siphoned off funds from Britannia's operations in India. An Indian court instructed Pillai to return the money he had allegedly taken from Britannia, or risk losing his directorship in Britannia Industries in India. After a bitter boardroom battle, Pillai was finally forced to cede control of Britannia to Groupe BSN.

Meanwhile, the Singapore court issued an arrest warrant for Pillai after finding him guilty of defrauding the local government of about $17.2 million. In a move involving high drama, Rajan escaped to India where he managed to get a stay on his extradition from a court in Kerala. Eventually, the Indian police arrested him from a hotel in Delhi in June 1995 and took him to Tihar Jail. A few days later, he was found dead in his cell under mysterious circumstances. His wife later alleged that jail officials had mistreated him and had neglected him when he fell ill in prison, causing his untimely demise.

Pillai was also credited with bringing back the Coca-Cola Company to India in 1993 after the US-based cola company was driven out in 1977 by the then central minister, George Fernandes, in the Morarji Desai government. The move earned Pillai praise from the media as well as the business community. But very soon the Coca-Cola Company shrugged off its alliance with Pillai, and started its own operations. If Rajan Pillai had tempered his ambition, he could have easily expanded his businesses and might have become one of the foremost businessmen in the country.

Though his friendship with Pillai was short-lived, Mallya continued his association with Janardhan Pillai's business in Kerala.

A United Breweries veteran says that until a decade after Mallya took over the UB Group, it was a transparent organization. Reviews were conducted professionally and there were strong processes in place.

An unwritten rule for a long time was that no matter what the price of a certain brand was, the gross percentage margin of each brand had to be maintained. It may not have boosted the top-line growth (revenues) dramatically, but it was good enough for the bottom line (profits) to remain healthy.

But once the management took the decision to make United Spirits the largest player in the world, the company's executives came under severe pressure to reach the target as quickly as possible. To achieve the milestone, a brand such as Kerala Malt whisky, a low-margin, high-volume product began to be pushed in the market even though it did not add much to the bottom line.

It wasn't very clear why a company would want to earn less in its race to become an industry leader. But later events showed that it was an attempt to window dress the company for higher valuation in the market.

~

Two years after his father passed away, Vijay married Sakina, whom he had met in Bombay through common friends, Ravi Jain and Nina Pillai. Sakina was a Bohra Muslim and worked as an air hostess. She converted to Hinduism before the marriage and took on the name Sameera. The marriage was performed in Goa and was followed by parties at the Mallyas' Neeladri bungalow in Bombay, and in Bangalore, Delhi and Calcutta.

In 1986, Sameera gave birth to Siddharth, Mallya's only son. By the early 1990s, Mallya and Sameera had filed for divorce. People close to Mallya claim that his preoccupation with his business caused a rift in their marriage. Despite the separation, Mallya saw to it that Sameera was well provided for.

Mallya married again. His second wife, Rekha, is the daughter of Kumar Siddana, a racehorse owner. Rekha and their daughters, Leena and Tanya, live in the US.

2

The Battle for Shaw Wallace

Vijay Mallya spent an entire night at the police commissioner's office on Infantry Road in Bangalore. He had been arrested on his way back from Calcutta on the night of 5 June 1985 for violating the Foreign Exchange Regulation Act (FERA).

With the exception of Allen Mendonca, an intrepid reporter who wrote about the incident in the *Indian Express*, the Bangalore press did not carry the story—either they did not get wind of the arrest or they chose not to report it. By the time the *Express* was out for circulation the next morning, the thirty-year-old Mallya had already been released with surety from one of his managers who had to furnish his home ownership papers to get his boss out of the police commissioner's office.

All transactions involving foreign currency at that time were put under a microscope because India didn't have a deep enough forex reserve to boast about. Such transactions had to be approved by the Reserve Bank of India and any violations were treated as criminal offences. Mallya had fallen afoul of the regulators, but few knew what was going on behind the scenes until he was arrested. (The second time Mallya faced arrest was in October 2012 when a cheque issued by his airline, Kingfisher Airlines, to the GMR Group, which operates the Hyderabad airport, bounced. A non-bailable arrest warrant was issued against Mallya and four others for failing to pay the user charges levied by the airport. Surprisingly, the charges were dropped and Mallya flew into India in time to be physically present to cheer his racing team, Sahara Force India, at the Formula 1 racing event.) Once the news of Mallya's night at the police commissioner's office broke, the national press was all over the story, trying to dig more and find out how Mallya got into this mess.

What unfolded was a sensational tale of corporate intrigue, double-crossing and family feuds—all centred on Shaw Wallace & Company. The battle for Shaw Wallace is an important chapter in the life of

Vijay Mallya. He spent the best part of his youth, and over two decades, fighting to gain control of a company which he had coveted since the day he took over the reins from his father. What is unique about this battle is that Mallya is perhaps one of the few corporate czars who bought the same company twice: once for Rs 55 crore and two decades later for a whopping Rs 1545 crore.

Shaw Wallace & Company was started in 1886 by UK-based Robert Gordon Shaw and Charles William Wallace, in Calcutta. The company owned tea gardens in east India, operated gas stations for Burmah Oil Company and even owned a few distilleries and breweries. Old-timers say that Shaw Wallace was one of the most ethical companies in its heyday and was very well managed. Long before employee stock-option plan became a buzzword, Shaw Wallace had introduced a similar scheme called the SW Staff Participation Trust for its employees. About 5–6 per cent of the company's profits was set aside for the trust. Shares from the trust were given out to senior employees to retain their services.

Such focus on employees and stakeholders had turned Shaw Wallace into a blue-chip company. Its return on capital was as high as 165 per cent during the 1970s and its debt on the books never lasted more than fifteen days. The first Indian chairman of Shaw Wallace was S. Panduranga Acharya who took over from Sir Anthony Hayward, after whom some of the brands were named.

Acharya began his career with Shaw Wallace as an assistant accountant, eventually becoming the chairman and managing director (CMD). He ran the company competently, though people who worked with him reckoned he was more of an accountant than a businessman. It is believed that even when there was enough cash for the company to expand and diversify, Acharya would tell his managers who routinely tipped him off about acquisition opportunities that he would rather put all the extra money in banks than invest it in acquiring assets. What worked for Shaw Wallace, however, was an enviable portfolio of liquor brands such as Royal Challenge, Haywards, Director's Special, Officer's Choice, Antiquity and Antiquity Blue, all which have stood the test of time. It had everything going for it—a clean record, high returns to shareholders, marquee brands and piles of cash—making it the perfect acquisition for the ambitious.

Shaw Wallace initially had multiple owners

through cross holding among the promoters. Sime Darby, based out of Malaysia, was one of the owners while R.G. Shaw Company, based in London, was another which held 40 per cent stake in Shaw Wallace. Both Sime Darby and Shaw Wallace had interlocking shares. In 1971, Sime Darby decided to take over R.G. Shaw's operations and did so through a reverse merger. The result was that Shaw Wallace came under the control of Sime Darby. But when Sime Darby decided to acquire the tyre-maker Dunlop in Malaysia, it decided to sell off its 40 per cent stake in Shaw Wallace to raise money for the acquisition. At that time, Shaw Wallace had assets of around Rs 6 crore and its turnover was Rs 200 crore.

Mallya, who had been eyeing Shaw Wallace for a long time, was thrilled to find out that the company's foreign shareholding was up for sale. But, according to domestic laws, since he was an Indian citizen, he was not allowed to acquire a company based abroad. To overcome the hurdle, he decided to rope in a business partner who was a non-resident Indian and hence was eligible to acquire the foreign shareholding of Shaw Wallace. As he didn't know any businessmen who were NRIs, he decided to tap into the network of his friend Brijesh Mathur who used to work at Grindlays Bank.

The brief to Mathur was simple: rope in an NRI businessman who would be willing to buy the foreign shareholding of Shaw Wallace and, once Mallya was able to get NRI status, transfer the shareholding to him. But then even the best-laid plans can sometimes go horribly wrong and in this case, they did. Of all the businessmen in the world, Mathur chose Manohar Rajaram Chhabria, a Sindhi businessman who had interests in electronics and a few other companies, to collaborate with Mallya. A non-resident India, the lanky Chhabria was as pugnacious as they come and was known for acquiring Indian companies which had foreign shareholding.

It is not known whether Mallya performed a background check on Chhabria before agreeing to partner with him; he seems to have had implicit faith in Mathur's judgement. Chhabria and Mallya met several times to go over the plan before deciding to put it into operation. They decided to float a joint venture which would be registered in Hong Kong for the purpose of acquiring Shaw Wallace. The company in turn would float a special purpose vehicle—Carrasco—in which the partners would have equal shareholding.

But Mallya was not the only businessman to know

about the potential sale of Shaw Wallace. The Canadian liquor major, Seagram Company, and the US-based cookie company, Nabisco, were also in the race to acquire Shaw Wallace. But at some point of time, Seagram either lost interest or delayed taking a firm decision on the bid even though it was a hot favourite to win the deal. Nabisco for some reason was not considered a serious contender. Eventually Sime Darby approached Mallya, asking him whether he was willing to raise the bid price. In his eagerness to buy Shaw Wallace, Mallya agreed to increase the price. Meanwhile, there were enough rumours doing the rounds that certain interests had paid off top executives at both Sime Darby and Seagram in an attempt to bag Shaw Wallace. But such rumours and more were bound to circulate because of the nature of the transaction, and were never substantiated.

Mallya had made two assumptions here: one that he would get his NRI status soon, which would ensure that he was not violating the laws of the land. The second assumption was that he would not face much resistance from the Indian management of Shaw Wallace or his proxy.

By now it seemed fairly certain that Mallya would win the bid. But what unfolded after this was a series of events which left Mallya wondering what on earth had made him partner with Chhabria. Sime Darby either did not know Indian regulations or didn't care for them. Acharya, the CMD of Shaw Wallace at the time the company was being sold, is believed to have received a call from one of the directors of Sime Darby informing him that they had sold off their entire stake to a company run by an Indian resident and an NRI. The news left Acharya stunned. He had nurtured Shaw Wallace to a position of strength and perhaps assumed that Sime Darby would offer the company to him first. Once it became clear that he had been completely sidestepped in the decision-making process, he decided that he wouldn't let go of the company without a fight. He also assumed that with the help of the financial institutions who were key shareholders in the company, he would be able to retain control of Shaw Wallace.

As per the deal with Sime Darby, all Mallya had to do now was raise about $26 million to buy the foreign shareholding in Shaw Wallace, which would give him majority control of the Calcutta-based company. To fund the acquisition, both Mallya and Chhabria decided that they would raise part of the money through debt while the rest—about

$6 million each—would come from their own contributions.

Here is where several versions emerge about the nature of the deal. According to one version, as the entire process of acquiring Shaw Wallace was conceived and executed by Mallya, the onus of paying the entire amount rested with him and not with Chhabria. But Mallya's hands were tied because he was yet to be granted NRI status. But mysteriously, the required funds were raised and Carrasco became the 40 per cent owner of Shaw Wallace. How did that happen? Around the same time, rumours started circulating in corporate circles that Mallya might have actually managed to pump in the $6 million.

There are also unsubstantiated rumours that it was Acharya and his men who actually tipped off the police in India about Mallya's alleged violation of forex laws. The police decided that a prima facie case could indeed be made against Mallya and he was promptly arrested when he arrived in Bangalore from Calcutta while Kishore Chhabria, Manu's brother who was also a director of the joint venture, was arrested in Delhi.

Though both of them were released on bail, Mallya's secret deal was now out in the open. But did

Mallya actually pay the money required to buy Shaw Wallace? If he did, then it was in clear violation of FERA rules.

Until Mallya roped him in, Manu Chhabria did not realize how lucrative and important a company Shaw Wallace was. Had it not been for Mallya, the Sindhi businessman wouldn't have got even a whiff of such a big company going abegging, as a close relative of Chabbria revealed later. It was pretty obvious that Chhabria would not let such a company slip out of his hands. He also realized that Mallya could never publicly admit that he was in bed with Chhabria for this deal.

Sensing a huge opportunity, the canny businessman did not leave it to Mallya to raise the additional money required to buy Shaw Wallace. He himself started approaching banks, and by January 1985, had managed to raise the required finances to acquire Shaw Wallace on his own.

With the officials from the Enforcement Directorate chasing him, Mallya had to eventually backtrack and let go of his stake in Carrasco, thereby handing over full control of the company to Chhabria.

The story might have ended with Chhabria

gaining control of Shaw Wallace had it not been for the tough legal battle put up by Acharya. Not to be left behind, Chhabria filed a counter case with the Department of Company Affairs under section 397 of the Companies Act alleging that Acharya should be removed from his position as CMD because of allegations of misappropriation and diversion of funds and for stripping of assets of the company.

The battle between the two lasted for over two years. During that period, Acharya managed to mop up about 17 per cent extra stake in the company; now he just needed the support of the financial institutions to topple Chhabria.

But at a crucial shareholders' meeting in 1987, which was called to decide the ownership issue, the financial institutions, which had always supported Acharya in the past, decided to abstain from voting for reasons best known to them. Chhabria won the vote and the company was in the bag. Acharya went back to his office and put in his papers, bringing to an end his more than three-decade-long association with Shaw Wallace. Subsequently, Acharya revealed to a journalist that Chhabria had graciously offered to let him continue as the CMD but he had declined the offer. Acharya now lives in Bangalore and is associated with several non-government organizations there.

Years later, expressing his condolences over the demise of Manu Chhabria in 2002, an *Economic Times* report quoted Acharya as saying that he fought to wrest back control of Shaw Wallace on the issue of principles. The acquisition of such a substantial stake should have taken place in a transparent manner, though he claimed that Sime Darby had informed him that the stake was in fact sold to a Bengali lawyer.

Once Chhabria was in the saddle, it was Mallya's turn to stake his claim. He demanded that Chhabria give him 50 per cent of the ownership of Shaw Wallace. But Chhabria declined, stating that since Mallya had not paid his part of the money fully, he could not assert part-ownership. Chhabria also reminded him that not only had Mallya maintained that he did not have any knowledge of the transaction and denied being a part-owner of Carrasco, he had also declared to the Enforcement Directorate in Bombay in August 1985 that he had no connection with either Chhabria or with Shaw Wallace.

Mallya wasn't chagrined with the fact that he had misjudged Chhabria. It was becoming increasingly clear that Mallya had not done his homework before launching his bid to acquire Shaw Wallace. When Chhabria refused to give him his share in Shaw Wallace, Mallya is believed to have asked him to return his money instead. But Chhabria told him that Mallya's share had been used up for paying legal fees.

There was no documentary evidence that could support Mallya's claim. Apparently, Chhabria used this loophole to inform Mallya that he never received any money from him.

A desperate Mallya is believed to have rushed to Delhi to seek intervention from politicians, hoping they would counsel Chhabria but nothing came of it.

Mallya had no other option but to bide his time till he was declared an NRI and, once economic reforms hit the country in the early 1990s, readied himself to fight the battle to wrest control of Shaw Wallace.

The court battle was fought in Hong Kong as that was where the takeover vehicle, Carrasco, was registered. It turned out to be a no-holds-barred corporate battle. Chhabria by then had increased his stake in Shaw Wallace to around 55 per cent. Of the remaining, 22 per cent was with the financial institutions, 7 per cent with foreign institutional investors and 16 per cent with the public. According to *Corporate Takeovers in India* by Vijay Kumar Kaushal, the shares of Shaw Wallace were held by R.G. Shaw and its three subsidiaries: Thomas Rice Milling Co. Ltd, Shaw Scott & Co. Ltd and Shaw Darby & Co. Ltd.

Kaushal claims that in order to acquire Shaw Wallace, Chhabria actually bought Carrasco through his Singapore company, Keysberg Ltd. In turn, Carrasco took a $15-million loan from the American Express Bank. The balance of $11.14 million was loaned to Carrasco by Chhabria with $9.67 million being given by Keysberg and $1.47 million directly funded by him. Carrasco, according to the books, was half owned by Chhabria, but the identity of the other part-owner was not known even then. It is believed that Mallya's stake apparently reflected in the transaction. American Express Bank which had extended a loan of $15 million to Carrasco, had done so based on the cash deposits Mallya made to the bank. But when the case came up for scrutiny after Mallya took Chhabria to court, Chhabria is believed to have disputed it by producing before the Indian Company Law Board a letter written by the vice president of the bank stating that the loan was arranged on a personal guarantee from R.R. Chhabria, a relative of Manu Chhabria.

Now that the trail regarding the $15 million had been established, the next component of the money—$9.67 million from Chhabria to Keysberg— came under scrutiny. Allegations were made that the money may have come to Carrasco from a $10.3-million loan that a Singaporean firm, Tentura Ltd, which has a management contract with a Far Eastern subsidiary of Mallya's United Breweries, took from the State Bank of India, Singapore.

Mallya denied that such a transaction had taken place and pointed out that $9 million out of the $10.3 million was drawn against letters of credit. He also claimed that he was being needlessly drawn into matters concerning Tentura and he had no financial links with the company. United Breweries' link to the firm was simply through a management contract.

Shaw Wallace was not Chhabria's only acquisition. His success emboldened him to acquire more companies, one of which was Dunlop Tyres which he bought in collaboration with R.P. Goenka but later, he fell out with him just as he had with Mallya.

This was how Indian corporate battles were fought then: under the cover of darkness and by exploiting the poor regulatory environment in India.

3

Shaw Wallace Again

Though Chhabria had successfully managed to ward off the threat from Acharya and was now in the saddle, he constantly worried about how Mallya would mount a bid to regain control of Shaw Wallace. After all, the entire takeover operation had been Mallya's brainchild and Chhabria was merely part of the supporting cast.

But Mallya knew it would not be easy to wrest control of Shaw Wallace because of the inherent complications in the way the deal was structured and executed. Therefore, he and the strategy cell of the company, decided that wisdom lay in bidding for Shaw Wallace's key brands. But this approach was not all that simple. After all, why would Chhabria part with marquee brands? Mallya persisted in the belief that there was no harm in trying either. A hostile bid for brands would create some amount of turbulence and raise suspicion in the rival's camp.

In 1999, Mallya made an offer to buy Royal Challenge, Director's Special and Haywards whiskies for about Rs 250 crore. These three were among the leading brands in their segments. Put in perspective, in 1985, Mallya was willing to pay Rs 55 crore ($27 million) to buy out Shaw Wallace itself and now he was willing to pay nearly five times more for just three brands in Shaw Wallace's portfolio. In fact, it was good money if Chhabria had agreed to sell the brands as he would have been able to wipe off some of the losses his group of companies had incurred.

But being an astute businessman, Chhabria realized what Mallya was up to. Now it was his turn to make a counter offer.

According to a report in the *Economic Times*, he hired an advertising agency to launch a campaign which would put Mallya in his place. The ad firm came out with a television commercial mocking Mallya's rather audacious offer. The commercial shows a bar in a club where a set of people are outshouting each other to buy different brands of liquor. A man walks in with a pronounced swagger, crushes a cigarette butt with his heel and goes up to the bartender, and says: 'I want to buy RC, DSP and Haywards.' Taken aback, the bartender blinks and exclaims: 'Vijay sahib, aap bhi?'

Then the camera zooms in on cartons of Director's Special and Royal Challenge placed near the bar, and the voiceover declares: 'India's most wanted.'

The ad apparently did dent Mallya's hopes of bagging the brands, though Chhabria later claimed that United Breweries Ltd never wanted to put money on the table. He confided to a journalist that if Mallya had been really keen, he would have considered the offer seriously.

Mallya's animosity towards Manu Chhabria was well known, but the liquor tycoon also had a falling out with Manu's brother, Kishore, later.

Even though Kishore and Manu Chhabria were siblings, there was no love lost between the two because of certain family misunderstandings. As a result, Kishore decided to part ways with his brother and walked away with one of the subsidiaries of Shaw Wallace, BDA Distilleries, a company with total revenues of about Rs 120 crore, after he had raised his stake in the subsidiary by buying shares in the market. Mallya, who was closely watching the developments in the Chhabria family, decided to approach Kishore, offering him a 26 per cent stake in one of his companies, Herbertsons, if he agreed to merge BDA with the company. Mallya had been eyeing BDA for some time because one of its brands, Officer's Choice whisky, was the largest-selling whisky in its segment.

There was another, much bigger, design behind his offer to Kishore Chhabria. Even though Kishore had walked away with BDA, Manu had filed a case against his brother to get back the company. Mallya realized that if Kishore were to lose the case, then BDA would go back to Manu, and Herbertsons would get a toehold in Chhabria's empire. Kishore took up Mallya's offer and was appointed vice chairman of Herbertsons. As per the deal, Mallya transferred 25.52 per cent of his 46.9 per cent stake in Herbertsons and 75,000 convertible debentures to Kishore Chhabria.

However, the friendship between Mallya and the younger Chhabria didn't last long, for Mallya learnt that Chhabria had started increasing his stake in Herbertsons by purchasing shares in the open market.

But Kishore Chhabria had a different take on the

dispute with Mallya. He claimed that Mallya had gone back on his promise of delegating more powers to him even though he was made the vice chairman of Herbertsons. Therefore, the only way for him to get a firm hold in Herbertsons was to increase his stake in the company through the open market. Between 1994 and 1997, Kishore Chhabria ended up acquiring another 20.27 per cent stake in Herbertsons. When Mallya learnt that Kishore was quietly buying more shares of Herbertsons, he increased his stake from the 21.38 per cent he had held earlier to 37.88 per cent through the open market route.

Some of these transactions were allegedly carried out in a manner frowned upon by regulators and lawmakers.

The matter was taken to court and, at one point, Mallya was battling both the brothers in different cases. Kishore Chhabria did offer a way out by stating that he would return the stake he held in Herbertsons if Mallya paid Rs 120 crore as well as cash against the stake that Chhabria owned. Obviously, Mallya would have none of it. The case continued and even went to the Supreme Court. SEBI then asked both of them to divest the wrongfully acquired stakes through a sale in the public. But by early 2005, both

Mallya and Kishore Chhabria realized that their long dispute would only drain them further and both of them went back to the negotiating table and settled their differences.

Kishore Chhabria withdrew from Herbertsons, selling his entire stake of slightly over 49 per cent to United Breweries, while Mallya handed back BDA Distilleries to Chhabria. The deal was finally settled for Rs 131 crore in favour of Kishore Chhabria. In turn, Mallya decided to consolidate his entire liquor business into one entity, United Spirits, while Kishore Chhabria decided to restructure BDA.

By 2000, the Chhabria brothers started reconciliation efforts and ended their decade-long rivalry. Shaw Wallace and Manu Chhabria withdrew all the 200 cases against Kishore Chhabria except one, which came back to haunt Kishore Chhabria later.

But tragedy struck the Chhabria family soon after. Manu Chhabria, who had been ailing for some time and had undergone a bypass surgery, passed away suddenly on 6 April 2002. Days before Chhabria passed away, Mallya is rumoured to have visited him at the hospital to inquire about his health.

Chhabria left his entire empire, the $1.5-billion Jumbo Group, to his wife, Vidya, and their three daughters, Kiran, Komal and Bhavika. India's first corporate raider was dead, but the conflict between Shaw Wallace and Mallya was not over. It took another three years and innumerable pitched battles fought in courts and boardrooms for it to come to an end.

Though Vidya Chhabria became the chairman of Shaw Wallace after her husband passed away, she did not have the experience required to run such a large business empire and her daughters too staked a claim for bigger shares for themselves. The family finally decided to exit several of their businesses and hive off Shaw Wallace into two entities: beer and liquor; and seek joint venture partners for both.

As soon as Mallya learnt that Shaw Wallace was seeking a joint venture partner, he decided to sue the company as the dispute over the ownership issue was still pending in the Hong Kong court. Also, one of his companies, McDowell, held a small stake in Shaw Wallace, which allowed him to file a case seeking to restrain the Chhabrias from hiving off the assets. He followed it up with an open offer for Shaw Wallace's liquor business.

In the case of Shaw Wallace's beer business, Mallya approached the Bombay High Court to restrain

South African Breweries (SABMiller), one of the bidders and the second-largest beer company in the world, from entering any deal with Shaw Wallace.

Though Mallya received flak for filing these cases, he maintained that he was doing so to protect the shareholders and creditors of Shaw Wallace. But why the UB Group would want to protect their interests was beyond one's imagination.

Mallya was clearly set to disrupt the business empire of Shaw Wallace and he hoped that repeated attempts to do so would unsettle the company's new bosses, including the chairperson Vidya Chhabria and the new managing director (MD) Komal Vazir Chhabria.

But the joint venture did happen and both Shaw Wallace and SABMiller entered into a 50–50 partnership. The South African company bought 50 per cent in the venture as well as management control for $132.8 million. At that time, Shaw Wallace had 22 breweries in its fold and sales of 32 million cases— about 36 per cent of the total market.

The reason SABMiller was allowed to proceed with the joint venture, which it eventually took over, was the fact that both Mallya and Vidya Chhabria decided to call a truce.

Two developments brought on their decision to shake hands: One, Mallya had won a major legal battle in the Hong Kong high court in January 2004, which upheld his contention that he was in fact an equal partner in Carrasco, the joint venture which had been floated to acquire Shaw Wallace. And, two, the Jumbo Group, which also owned Shaw Wallace, decided to challenge the order and refer the matter to a court of appeal as it felt that it 'clearly constitutes criminal breach of the Indian law'.

In view of these interminable cases, Vidya Chhabria decided to use her discretion and end one of the biggest corporate battles in India by agreeing to a settlement with Mallya. So, in 2004, both United Breweries Ltd and Shaw Wallace made a public announcement that all disputes between them had been resolved. The case in the Hong Kong court was dismissed in June 2004 once they filed consent terms.

But what had not been resolved yet was who would get to partner with Shaw Wallace in their liquor business.

As Shaw Wallace had already found a partner for its beer business, it decided to call for bids for its liquor business in 2004. Mallya was quick to realize that though both he and the Chhabrias had agreed to settle all legal disputes, he was not exactly welcome in their fold. The settlement was to ensure that Mallya never again troubled the Chhabrias. But having lost the initial battle to take over Shaw Wallace, Mallya could not let go of the opportunity to have another shot at acquiring it. This time, he also had the added advantage of not having Manu Chhabria as an adversary.

He put in a bid for the liquor business for Rs 1251 crore. The other bidders were Newbridge Capital in partnership with Ramesh Vangal, the former head of Seagram India, and Whyte & Mackay. As it turned out, United Breweries' bid was the highest, a fact which Mallya claimed had been orally conveyed to him by McKinsey, advisers to Shaw Wallace. He also claimed that he was informed that the bid was for the 55 per cent stake held by the Chhabria family and not for the liquor business.

But the last thing the Chhabrias wanted was to let the company go to Mallya after putting up a stiff resistance for over two decades. Even though the bid was accepted, Shaw Wallace decided that it would delay the sale of the business for as long as possible.

However, Mallya was not one to give up easily. He returned the following year, in February 2005, with an open offer to acquire 25 per cent of the stake at a price of Rs 250 per share. It meant shelling out a total of Rs 300 crore if the offer was fully subscribed, valuing the company at Rs 1200 crore. It was an audacious move but one that would give him rich dividends if it paid off.

Shaw Wallace was quick to respond to the open offer, terming it as a hostile bid that did not have the consent of the promoters. But Mallya clarified that as the bidding process was taking a long time, he had decided to make the open offer through his three companies—United Spirits, McDowell & Co., and Phipson Distillery.

Of course, one obvious benefit for Mallya was that if he acquired Shaw Wallace, his company would emerge as a major spirits company in the world with total sales of 53 million cases, including 15 million cases of Shaw Wallace. Also, even if Mallya owned part of the 25 per cent he had made, he would be an indirect owner of Shaw Wallace's beer business, partly owned by SAB Miller, and be a significant minority shareholder with the power to prevent Shaw Wallace from initiating the sale of the liquor business to anyone without his approval.

As the days went by, Mallya's pressure tactics via

the open offer started working. His stance that he would talk only to Vidya Chhabria and not to her daughters also worked in his favour.

In March 2005, he received word from the Vidya Chhabria camp suggesting that she was ready to give in. Mallya arrived in Dubai and, after several meetings with her, managed to convince her to part with Shaw Wallace.

It is believed that the then ICICI Bank chief, K.V. Kamath, brokered the deal which was finalized for $300 million—Rs 1300 crore. Soon after the deal was signed, Mallya called his mother who was living in London at the time to inform her that he had finally bagged the Shaw Wallace liquor business.

A very pleased Lalitha Mallya congratulated her son on his latest conquest.

The final outgo for the UB Group was Rs 1545 crore, including Rs 312 crore for the 25 per cent stake through the open offer. ICICI Bank facilitated the entire funding.

As Mallya had already made it clear that he was not interested in Shaw Wallace's beer business, SABMiller later bought the remaining stake of 50 per cent by paying another Rs 158 crore ($36 million) to acquire 99 per cent of the beer business.

Shaw Wallace was later merged with United Spirits. This ended one of the biggest battles in corporate India.

'It's been twenty years, three months and four days, to be precise, since I set my sight on Shaw Wallace. It was a battle worth it and today, I have handsomely won it,' Vijay Mallya declared at a press conference later.

But Mallya had a few more scores to settle still. This time, he trained his guns at his foe-turned-friend-turned-foe Kishore Chhabria. In 2006, a year after he acquired Shaw Wallace, he filed a case against the Kishore Chhabria-owned BDA Distilleries, seeking the return of its Officer's Choice whisky.

Now how could he do that when he had already allowed Kishore Chhabria to take BDA Distilleries with him in return for shares in Herbertsons? It was because, out of the 200-odd cases which Manu Chhabria had filed through Shaw Wallace against his brother, Kishore, the one relating to Officer's Choice was still pending in the court. It was either an oversight or deliberate, but Mallya made use of it once Shaw Wallace was in his kitty.

After a series of long-drawn battles which stretched for a decade and a half, Mallya decided to end his dispute with Kishore Chhabria. More because he was set to finalize the deal with Diageo (which would take over United Spirits) and did not want any litigations to delay the process.

In October 2012, Mallya agreed to withdraw all cases relating to the legal dispute over the brand. In return, he received a sum of Rs 8 crore—approximately $2 million—from Kishore Chhabria for doing so.

That ended all disputes with the Chhabria family. Unless Mallya chooses to spring another one.

4

The MCF Story

'You have an option but no choice,' declared Mallya with a finality which was typical of him.

The thirty-something official of the UB Group knew right away that the decision had been made for him. Mallya had offered him a posting to one of his group companies, Mangalore Chemicals & Fertilizers (MCF), which he had recently acquired from the Karnataka government. He could still opt out but that meant opting out of the group itself. But he knew he was far from taking that step. After all, Mallya had treated him well in the company. He had shown his trust in him when he had put him on a key assignment which involved the acquisition of a distillery in Nashik, just a few years after he had joined the group from the pharma company Astra-IDL (now Astra-Zeneca).

'I like what I see,' Mallya had remarked to his friend and chief financial officer (CFO), Naresh Malhotra, after meeting Darius Mehta during his recruitment.

Most people might assume that the liquor business in India does not call for IIT graduates or chartered accountants as employees because of the perception that almost everything gets done under the table. Traditionally, this was how liquor companies did their business, but all of that changed because of the Mallyas. They hired smart, well-educated, well-turned-out people who reflected their vision of creating a professional image for the industry.

Vijay Mallya didn't just stop at hiring them. He paid them well and even allowed people at the helm of affairs to run their units or businesses without any interference. The official returned home that evening to discuss the new turn of events with his wife who had assumed that her husband would ask her to start packing for London. Mallya had initially offered him a posting to the UB Group's London office as its head.

Mallya had bought at a throwaway price the ailing Mangalore Chemicals & Fertilizers which he felt could be turned around in three years. Many say it was his connection with the state government which got him the company. 'You know I can smell profits in three years,' Mallya confided to the official after he had agreed to join MCF. He had managed to put together a team of five who he believed would be able to pull the company out of the rut.

Why would Mallya want to get into the fertilizer business of all things in the world? Because it was a business protected by the government. Fertilizer prices are controlled by the government which may mean lower profits all year round because the industry is seen as an entity which carries out social service in the larger interest of a nation where agriculture is the mainstay of the people.

Cultivating the image of someone who was sensitive to the social needs of the country was important for Mallya who, at that time, nurtured ambitions of becoming a member of Parliament.

The MCF story needs to be told though it may not be fashionable to own such a company. It is also perhaps the only listed major company which is unrelated to the core business of the UB Group and has not closed down yet.

From its initial days, its growth and turnaround, it is clear that Mallya mostly got the right people to head his companies. When Mallya acquired MCF, it was an ailing public-sector company, which got off to a wrong start from the very beginning. The Tatas had bought the licence to run MCF in 1969 from Duggal Enterprises, a north Indian company, and handed over the company to one of their most trusted lieutenants, P.A. Narielwala, whose apparent closeness to India's first prime minister, Jawaharlal Nehru, was well known. It was said that Indira Gandhi used to address Narielwala as 'uncle' and he fondly called her 'beti'.

The MCF project was started on the assumption that the Karnataka government would not fail to deliver on its promises of supplying water and power. However, neither promise could be kept because the nearby Gurpur river would dry up during the summer months, rendering the plant without adequate water for several months. Power was always an issue with the state and was considered more an election promise than anything else.

The project finally took off in 1971 and it took nearly six years for the company to start production and, by that time, time and cost overruns had multiplied. Unfortunately, the plant had to be shut down soon after it was commissioned because of inadequate supply of water. The shutdowns continued regularly thereafter.

It is suicidal for a fertilizer plant to keep shutting down because every closure leads to what is known as a thermal shock. In other words, shutting down a plant leads to temperature fluctuation causing stress to the plant machinery. Repeated shocks ultimately cripple the plant. The Tatas were helpless but the final blow came when the Karnataka government decided that the Tatas should not be part of the project any more. The show of no confidence was enough for Narielwala to quit and move back to his parent company. The MCF plant continued to be riddled with problems: it was overstaffed and had multiple unions which kept calling for strikes at the drop of a hat.

India being an agriculture-led economy, fertilizer prices are controlled by the government to keep farmers insulated from any fluctuation in the rates. This sometimes acts as a deterrent for a private company but Mallya did not seem to mind such shortcomings. In some ways, parallels could be drawn to his airline venture as well. Mallya knew that aviation turbine fuel was heavily taxed by the respective state governments but he still went ahead and got into the airline business.

'But you don't think like an entrepreneur,' Mallya had told a top official when he asked him why he was taking the risk of running a fertilizer company.

Unable to sustain the operations any longer, the Karnataka government decided to privatize and put MCF up for bidding, which was won by Mallya. The government was also happy to sell the company to a Kannadiga.

The structuring of the deal itself was a bit complex. Mallya was asked to infuse capital of Rs 10 crore into MCF to gain control of the company. It did look like a steal because the turnover of the company was as much as Rs 200 crore during 1990 itself. But it came with a lot of baggage. It had huge assets but was weighed down heavily with an enormous debt of Rs 162 crore which the government owed to twenty-two banks and financial institutions. As if this was not enough, the government had done a debilitating lease: it had sold off the dead diammonium phosphate plant which was being run with Japanese technology and bought it back through lease transactions with eight local leasing companies. The government paid Rs 32 crore for a Rs 26-crore plant and showed it as a sale and took it as revenue and declared a dividend as well.

In spite of such financial mismanagement, Mallya was brave enough to pick up over 30 per cent stake in the company. To turnaround the fortunes of the company, he put together a five-member team which insiders said was more like a five-member rescue mission.

The 'rescue mission' was led by the former CMD of Fertilisers and Chemicals, Travancore Ltd, N.B. Chandran, who was credited with turning around the company. The other members of the rescue team consisted of representatives from departments across the company. Soon after the UB Group took over the company in 1991, it was hit by a series of strikes by the employees. The then chief minister H.D. Deve Gowda called for a meeting between the employees' union and the management. It was decided at the meeting, that the management should restart the factory within a few days and pay strike wages as well. The UB Group, however, refused to dole out more cash, saying the company would have to raise funds on its own or allow it to sink. By then, banks too refused to lend further which eventually resulted in the company turning sick. The management was then forced to refer it to the Board for Industrial and Financial Reconstruction (BIFR). Companies which are referred to the BIFR are either sold off, closed down after their assets are stripped off to pay off debtors, or nursed back to health under the strict supervision of the government officials.

Even while MCF was limping from one crisis to another, Chandran's health had started deteriorating. In spite of the fact that he hardly attended office, Mallya never once hinted that Chandran should resign. But after a rather acrimonious annual general meeting where the union leader accused Chandran of corruption, his health deteriorated further and he passed away in October 1996.

Days later, Mallya appointed Darius Mehta as the MD and assigned to him the huge task of getting MCF out of the BIFR. Even though Mehta was more of an accountant than someone who had knowledge of running a manufacturing plant, he managed to convince the employees' unions (there were several of them) to allow the workers to resume work. Mallya on his part never interfered in the day-to-day working of the company but whenever needed would use his influence to get government clearances or even help raise funds.

At one point, he used his considerable clout to get UTI Bank (now Axis Bank) a Rs 40-crore working-capital loan for which UB Ltd stood a guarantor after other banks had refused to extend any loan.

MCF was on a stable wicket after that. However, some of the members of the crack team which was part of the revival of the company left in quick succession due to differences with the management. Much later, MCF was back in the news when there was talk about the possible sale of the company even as Mallya tried to source extra cash to pay off his debtors. Mallya has not been able to find a suitor so far and the company continues to remain with the UB Group.

However, Mallya is not the largest shareholder in MCF any more. Deepak Fertilisers and Petrochemicals Corporation Ltd has acquired a total of 24.4 per cent through market purchases while Mallya has about 21 per cent stake, and the Calcutta-based Zuari Fertilisers owns 16 per cent. Sailesh Mehta, owner of the Pune-based Deepak Fertilisers, has repeatedly said that he wants to increase the company's stake in MCF but only if Mallya agrees to let him do so. In case Mallya does agree, then Deepak Fertilisers could own as much as 51 per cent after an open offer, effectively ending the reign of the UB Group.

5

The Sword of Tipu Sultan

The auction was not without its share of
controversies. After all, the belongings of Mahatma
Gandhi which included the iconic round-rimmed
spectacles were on auction. The Indian government
wasn't exactly happy about the auction and tried to
stop it, even bringing a court injunction against it.
As a policy, the government does not participate in
any auctions as it believes it is tantamount to
gambling.

But being someone who sponsors the derby
regularly, Vijay Mallya clearly saw things differently
when he decided to bid for the precious belongings
of Mahatma Gandhi. The Mahatma had gifted these
articles to the Raja of Junagarh in the 1930s much
before he wrote his will.

'Let's go for it, Tony,' Mallya had told his friend and colleague Tony Bedi, the president of the US operations of the UB Group.

The auction, being held by Antiquorum Auctioneers, famous for selling timepieces, started in earnest on the morning of 5 March 2009 at 595 Madison Avenue, New York. The collections, consisting of steel-framed spectacles, a pair of sandals, a bowl, a plate and a pocket watch, were owned by US film-maker and peace activist James Otis. But Otis, wasn't very happy auctioning the articles. He had even employed a lawyer to stop their sale but because he had signed a legally binding agreement with the auctioneers, it was impossible to withdraw at this stage. Otis was even willing to offer the entire collection to the Indian government, provided it agreed to some of his conditions which included holding a public exhibition of the articles as well as increasing the government spending for the poor.

The auctions began right on time. Lot 364 consisting of the Mahatma's belongings came up for auction by mid-afternoon and a hectic round of bidding started. Soon, the $1-million mark was breached which left just Mallya and former Indian cricket spinner Dilip Doshi in the fray. Doshi had entered the bid hoping to return the belongings to India. Mallya too wanted to do the same.

Mallya finally won the bid at $1.8 million and took possession of the belongings of a person who had advocated abstinence from liquor all his life. But once he won the bid, the Indian government claimed that it had in fact asked Mallya to buy these articles on its behalf. But Mallya quickly refuted any such communication stating that he bid on his own and the government had no part to play in it.

This was the second time Mallya had bid in an auction to take possession of an important piece of history.

~

'I am the mysterious buyer,' Mallya declared in a rather dramatic manner at a press conference in April 2004 in Bangalore. The item in question was the sword of the eighteenth-century ruler of Mysore, Tipu Sultan.

After making the announcement, Mallya grandly unveiled the 200-year-old sword, which he had bought at an auction in London for about Rs 1.5 crore, in front of gaping journalists.

Mallya seems to have a fetish for such things or maybe a heightened sense of nationalism. His own home on the swanky Vittal Mallya Road is full of artefacts, old paintings and antiques, though now it is being demolished to build an apartment complex. He even has a website called mallyacollection.com which gives details of all his collections, including an impressive array of vintage as well as state-of-the-art cars. According to the website, Mallya's collection includes a 1913 model Rolls-Royce Silver Ghost, a 1917 Harley Davidson, a 1926 version Mercedes and a Ferrari 1990 bicycle, three Ferraris and a McLaren.

Mallya's public revelation came six months after the 42-inch sword bearing a calligraphed hilt and its silver scabbard were bought. Critics immediately lashed out at him, stating that he bought the articles to garner more votes for the soon-to-be-held parliamentary elections.

'It is no gimmick,' Mallya, who was the president of the Janata Party, thundered, affronted by the questions suspecting his intentions. 'I bought it for the Kannadigas,' he replied. Critics remained unconvinced of his assertions that he had not bought the sword to gain political mileage.

Media reactions were tepid but no one could deny the fact that an Indian had indeed spent good money to buy back what rightfully belonged to the country. Tipu Sultan is highly respected in India for fighting against the British. It took almost forty years for the British to conquer Mysore, situated in south India, because of the stiff fight put up by Tipu and his father. Tipu died fighting the British in Srirangapatna on the banks of the Cauvery river near Mysore in 1799. The British took back his sword to London where it was given to General David Baird in recognition of his bravery against the Sultan.

In 2005, Mallya again bid for another set of items belonging to Tipu Sultan and won the right to own them. These included a silver-mounted flintlock sporting gun from Tipu's personal armoury and some thirty-odd items, for about Rs 9.7 crore.

But getting these articles was just one part of the story. The Government of India refused to waive the duty off if they were brought into India. Some of these articles are in the US and in the custody of Mallya. The liquor baron has promised to bring them back to India as and when the government waives off the duty.

6

The Politician

It was an unusually windy day. But the pilot ferrying Mallya, the 'working' president of the Janata Party, was confident that his MD 600-N machine, considered one of the safest copters in the world, was robust enough to handle such gusty weather conditions.

Mallya was on a whistle-stop tour of the northern districts of Karnataka to address a series of political rallies there. He had recently taken over as the working president of the dormant Janata Party in order to realize his political ambitions. The rallies were part of the election campaign leading up to the 2004 Karnataka state assembly polls.

Apart from Mallya, the others travelling in the six-seater copter were his political secretary, Tushita

Patel, film star Sanjay Khan and Ajmal Jamai, a cameraman of a television channel.

After the helicopter, which was on loan from Tata Tea for the election campaign, had taken off from Hubli, in north Karnataka, the pilot realized that the weather had worsened. He would need all his experience to get through this. As the copter approached the helipad near Bagalkot, a sudden gust of wind shook it uncontrollably and that's when the pilot decided to take evasive action by taking a sharp turn to the right. However, the sudden turn coupled with strong winds must have been too much even for a robust machine to keep itself on course. Realizing that something had gone wrong, Mallya shouted to the pilot: 'Pull the left rudder up, pull the left rudder up!' but by then it was too late; the copter was already spinning out of control.

The crowd gathered near the makeshift helipad inside a field to welcome Mallya watched in horror the copter tumbling down. Within minutes, the copter hit the ground with a huge thud and broke into two.

C.B. Yeshvanth Kumar, Mallya's press secretary who was waiting for the liquor baron's arrival near the fleet of vehicles lined up less than a kilometre away on the other side of field, saw people running towards the helipad shouting that the copter had crash-landed. Kumar couldn't believe his ears. Fighting panic, Kumar too started running towards the helipad, expecting the helicopter to burst into flames any moment. As he neared the crashed helicopter he was stunned to see Mallya outside it and looking around. Kumar later gathered that the only person who didn't lose his cool as the copter was hurtling towards the ground was Mallya. After being treated at a local government hospital for minor leg injuries, Mallya resumed his election campaign later in the evening.

Mallya and his co-passengers had survived miraculously. All of them had escaped with minor injuries probably because the copter's tail had hit the ground first and hence had acted as a shock absorber. But still, the outcome of the crash could have been worse.

The liquor baron was, however, convinced that one of the reasons he survived was his abiding faith in God. Inspite of all his flamboyance Mallya is a very god-fearing and superstitious person. A former executive in his company recalls that Mallya had once trimmed his goatee in such a way that it looked like the trunk of Lord Ganesha and kept showing it to his friends. Mallya also makes it a point to visit the temple of Lord Ayyappa in Sabarimala, Kerala, every year. Lord Ayyappa is a Hindu god, believed to be an incarnation of Lord Dharma Sastha, an offspring of Shiva and Vishnu (as Mohini, his female avatar).

Also, every new aircraft inducted into the Kingfisher fleet is flown down to Tirupathi, the abode of Lord Venkateshwara, before it is deployed into service.

Mallya is also known to perform several homas, a fire ritual which is an important Hindu ceremony to trigger various positive energies by making offerings to various gods and goddesses. On one occasion, he donated gold-plated doors worth Rs 80 lakh to the temple of Lord Subramanya, the lord of serpents, at Kukke Subramanya situated in south Karnataka.

Though Mallya survived the helicopter crash, his party was not so lucky during the 2004 elections. It could not even win a single seat, putting paid to his political ambitions. Mallya was already an independent member of the Rajya Sabha, the upper house of Parliament, when he took over as the national working president of the Janata Party. Once his party lost the elections in Karnataka, Mallya distanced himself completely. Mallya had joined politics sometime in 2000 but either couldn't give it enough time or was too naive to understand its intricacies. It is one thing to know politicians and quite another to be a politician.

Ten years later, the president of the Janata Party, Subramaniam Swamy, sacked Mallya from the post of working president, stating he was more of a 'sleeping, non-working' president.

Mallya, however, continues to be an independent member of the Rajya Sabha having won the seat from Karnataka for the second time with the help of 'friendly' political parties.

7

Kingfisher Airlines

'The worst sort of business is one that grows rapidly, requires significant capital to engender the growth, and then earns little or no money. Think airlines. Here a durable competitive advantage has proven elusive ever since the days of the Wright Brothers. Indeed, if a farsighted capitalist had been present at Kitty Hawk, he would have done his successors a huge favor by shooting Orville down. The airline industry's demand for capital ever since that first flight has been insatiable. Investors have poured money into a bottomless pit, attracted by growth when they should have been repelled by it. And I, to my shame, participated in this foolishness when I had Berkshire buy US Air preferred stock in 1989. As the ink was drying on our check, the company went into a tailspin, and before long our preferred dividend was no longer being paid. But we then got very lucky. In one of the recurrent, but always misguided, bursts of optimism for airlines, we were actually able to sell our shares in 1998 for a hefty gain. In the decade following our sale, the company went bankrupt.'

—Warren Buffet in a note to his shareholders

The traffic on Residency Road in Central Business District, Bangalore, was unusually light. It is typical for cars to be stuck in second gear when travelling the stretch connecting Residency Road to Vittal Mallya Road. The thin traffic was incentive enough for Ravi Nedungadi's chauffeur to floor the accelerator in his Mercedes.

Inside the car, the normally unflappable Nedungadi was getting a bit tense as he conversed with someone over his mobile.

He had been on the phone throughout the journey from his apartment on Hosur Road to the UB Group's headquarters. The phone was stuck to his ear even on the ride up the elevator to his sprawling tenth-floor office which overlooked Cubbon Park.

He ended his call as he entered his office. The

*conversation over the phone had got Nedungadi a
bit worried but before he could gather his thoughts,
Mallya barged into his room: 'So? Are we ready to
make the announcement?' asked Mallya.*

*Nedungadi had joined as corporate treasurer in
the UB Group in 1990 from Macneill & Magor
Ltd, a tea company. A genius with numbers, he
rose quickly through the ranks and in less than
fourteen years, had become the president and CFO
of the group.*

*Over the years it had become quite obvious that
Mallya had more confidence in him than anyone
else in his group. But Mallya's decision to enter the
airline sector had Nedungadi worried. The caller
at the other end was a big name in the airline
industry and had told him that the Indian
government policies weren't conducive enough to
invest in the sector.*

*Mallya was clearly a man in a hurry. As his
childhood friend and now the CMD of Biocon,
Kiran Mazumdar Shaw, had once remarked, 'He
listens to me and even consults me on important
issues. But he is his own man and he ought to be,
considering the fact that he now owns a business
spanning several continents.' Much before
Nedungadi had arrived at his office on the morning
of 15 November 2004, Mallya was already in his*

office, busy making calls. The first call was to a top executive in a private-sector bank who had stood by United Breweries for several years. But the conversation did not go as planned. The person at the other end kept arguing against Mallya's proposed project. Finally losing patience, Mallya cut the banker short by telling him that he didn't need his money anyway.

The next call was more important. It was to Kiran Rao, the Airbus representative for India.

Rao had studied at the prestigious Bishop Cotton School, a stone's throw away from Mallya's house. 'Okay, I will come over to Toulouse [Airbus headquarters]. But you know the deal, right?' Mallya was forthright.

Mallya indicated to him that he would need at least ten Airbus A320s and three A319s in the first two years, and that he was willing to spend over $1 billion to get them. Kiran Rao knew that if the deal did go through, Airbus would pip its bitter rival, Boeing, to the pole position.

It was after this call that Mallya hurried out of his office and barged into Nedungadi's room. The board meeting that afternoon was merely a couple of hours away.

'Vijay, maybe we should go over it again. We have made acquisitions fairly recently and we need

to settle down a bit,' Nedungadi put across his opinion as gently as possible.

So, this is it, thought Mallya to himself. It looks like Ravi has had a sudden attack of cold feet. But this wasn't going to stop him from moving ahead. 'Let us go ahead, Ravi. I know what we are getting into,' Mallya said, and walked out of the office, telling him that he would see him at the board meeting.

Nedungadi knew Mallya would not change his mind now. The board meeting of United Distilleries was uneventful. The MD, V.K. Rekhi, went on and on about how they had cornered the Scotch Whisky Association (SWA). 'The SWA won't bother us for a few years,' Rekhi remarked, and exchanged smiles with Mallya who was sitting at the head of the table. On his right sat the vice chairman of the group, Subhash Gupte.

The suave-looking Gupte had been the acting CMD of India's official carrier, Air India, before joining the UB Group. Mallya had roped in Gupte, who had over twenty-five years' experience as an airline professional, for his management skills. Gupte had also secretly nurtured his dream of launching an airline himself but didn't have the required resources to do so.

The Scotland-based SWA was turning out to be

a pain for the group's whisky business. It had threatened to drag the Indian government to the World Trade Organization for unfair trade practices. The government was levying a 300 per cent tax on Scotch whisky while the locally made whiskies got away with far lower taxes, making them much cheaper to buy.

Just as the interest among those seated in the boardroom was waning, Mallya waved his hand in the air. 'All right. I have an announcement to make. We have decided to float an airline venture,' Mallya declared rather abruptly. Everyone in the room went silent, trying to grasp the import of the announcement. After a rather long silence, Kalyan Ganguly, Mallya's friend and the MD of United Breweries, blurted out a question: 'Again, Vijay?' Ganguly's tone indicated that he was concerned.

Mallya had floated a company called UB Air in the late 1980s in the hope that the Indian government would allow him to carry out commercial operations one day. But when the government opened up the skies to the private airlines, Mallya was busy with his battle with the Chhabrias to wrest control of Shaw Wallace.

UB Air, however, continued to provide charter services for corporates as well as affluent individuals.

After some years, UB Air went into hibernation but Mallya's interest in starting an airline had not. In 1995, he set up another airline company and registered it in the name of Kingfisher Airlines with its corporate office in Bombay. It had remained a shell company till Mallya made that historic announcement.

'Yup. We will start operations on Siddharth's birthday. It is my gift to him,' said Mallya in a tone that indicated that the decision had been made. It was the first time Mallya had ever mentioned Siddharth's name at a board meeting. Unlike most family-run businesses where family members find a place on the board of the management, members of the Mallya family, with the exception of Siddharth Mallya, do not hold any positions on the board.

Even before Mallya revealed his plans for launching the airline to the board, he had started putting together a financial plan for the project. One of the first persons he met in this connection was the industrious Kiran Rao. Both decided to meet in Mallya's office in Bombay. Rao's major success in India was selling aircraft to sericulture-farmer-turned-entrepreneur Captain G.R. Gopinath who had placed orders for A320s to kick-start Air

Deccan. His business model was based on keeping the price of air tickets as low as possible so that more people could fly, drawing even those who had never flown before.

Rao had realized that selling aircraft in India was not as easy as selling them in the rest of the world. One had to strike a personal relationship with the airline's owner to get anywhere near selling even a single aircraft. In one of his presentations to the board of Airbus in Toulouse, France, Rao had explained: 'You sold aircraft to Vijay, Naresh [Goyal of Jet Airways] and Gopi [Captain Gopinath], not to the airlines themselves. In Europe, you sold aircraft to the Lufthansas of the world.' But if you could sell aircraft in India, you could sell them anywhere.

In India, Rao found out it was not necessary for a person to have some knowledge about the industry to start an airline. If a farmer could start one, a liquor baron with far better resources could start an airline too.

These thoughts kept running through his mind as he patiently waited for Mallya to appear in the United Breweries office. 'Just like anyone else, I was also meted out that special Mallya treatment,' Rao remarked later. The special Mallya treatment meant having to wait a long while until the man arrived grandly for the meeting, in this case three hours late.

Journalists tracking his group companies put up with such delays because they were assured of a good copy. Mallya's quotes and announcements most often made it to the front page of the newspapers and therefore editors were more than willing to hold back putting the newspaper to bed (printing) till the reporters filed their Mallya story.

Owners of bigger and more diversified corporate groups never received the same attention and space in the newspapers. Mallya was a phenomenon, never seen before in the corporate world. His charm, flamboyance, even arrogance, and his association with models and movie stars had made him a very colourful personality. Almost every middle-class Indian secretly aspired to lead his kind of life.

Mallya knew his importance to the media very well and milked it to his advantage. Even at the worst of times, nobody ever questioned him for keeping them waiting.

Rao's amusement at being asked to wait soon turned to irritation. Thankfully, his years of working as a salesman for Airbus had prepared him for situations like these. Rao had received a doctorate in aeronautical engineering from the University of London, on a scholarship from British Aerospace.

When he chose marketing over engineering as a career at Airbus, the choice was seen as a bit unusual considering the fact that the engineers were viewed with far greater respect at that time. However, for someone who made friends easily, it seemed an appropriate choice. Rao found immediate success in his job. Working along with John Leahy, who eventually became the chief operating officer at Airbus Industrie, Rao was able to swing key deals for the aircraft maker in the US. Impressed by his success Airbus sent him to India, one of the most difficult markets to crack open in the world for the company. Not for Boeing though. It was all over the place there. Among the few aircraft which Airbus had sold in India, one of them, an A320, belonging to the state-owned Indian Airlines, had been involved in an accident in Bangalore in 1990 which killed ninety-two people on board, including both the pilots. A rather stunned government had decided to ground all the A320s in the fleet.

It was sometime in the afternoon, much later than the scheduled meeting, that Mallya finally arrived. He immediately apologized to Rao, something he rarely did when he made journalists wait. But then Rao was key to his business plans. They chatted for some time, exchanging notes about Bangalore where Rao had studied at Bishop Cotton School, one of the elite schools in the city. Rao came back impressed, having forgotten the long wait he had had to put up with. 'Mallya and I became instant friends. We spent a lot of time developing the plans for the airline. He is one of the nicest people you will ever meet.'

Building a relationship with Mallya was important for Rao. Else, he might have lost out on a large order to his Boeing counterpart, Dinesh Keskar.

'Once you sell here, it doesn't stop. You need to strike personal relationships with the owners of the airlines,' Rao later said. Narrating an incident to a journalist in an interview, Rao recalled how an Airbus aircraft was hit by a truck at an airport in India. 'My family and I were holidaying at that time. It was a day after Christmas. I received a call from the owner of the airline asking me to fix the problem. My wife was amused. She said, "Kiran, you don't even have a toolbox."' But the problem had to be fixed. Rao got all the necessary people rounded up, who just about managed to get the aircraft to fly in time.

Impressed with Rao's sales pitch, Mallya flew down to the Airbus headquarters in Toulouse, the fourth largest city in France, to sign the deal. On 25 April 2005, Kingfisher Airlines took delivery of its first, brand-new Airbus A320 aircraft at a ceremony at the Airbus factory. The aircraft, according to the press statement released by the airline on that occasion, was equipped with an advanced in-flight entertainment system that offers a personal video screen at every seat with ten audio and five video channels. It was unique all right, the first in the history of Indian aviation. The entertainment options seemed revolutionary at a time when most airlines used to give away a free copy of their in-house magazine or a few newspapers to the passengers to keep them entertained and busy. In addition, the aircraft came equipped with an advanced Airborne Communications Addressing and Reporting System—ACARS—which enables better communication between the crew and the ground staff to enable better management all round. Clearly, Kingfisher was all set to redefine flying in India.

The A320 was part of a larger order which entailed the delivery of one such aircraft every month for the remainder of 2005.

The Launch

D-day was approaching fast. Mallya had tried very hard to get all the necessary clearances for the airline's maiden flight on 7 May 2005, his son's eighteenth birthday, but bureaucratic hassles had forced him to put it off to 9 May.

A day before the launch, Mallya had thrown a huge party in Bombay which saw a mix of the glitterati and the decision-makers in attendance. The next day, Mallya's hand-picked invitees, the who's who in the world of politics and industry, boarded Kingfisher Airlines' maiden flight to Bangalore. Some of the invitees included the then Union civil aviation minister, Praful Patel, and V. Thulasidas, MD of the state-owned carrier, Air India.

The flight to Bangalore gave a glimpse of the kind of service that Mallya would offer his passengers.

The upholstery was red and the rear of each seat was fitted with a small TV screen. The passengers were escorted to their seats by smartly turned out air hostesses who were easy on the eyes and, more importantly, broke into a smile when they saw you. Once seated, the passengers were given a small zipped pouch which contained a headphone, eye mask, pen, and tissue paper. Soon after, a fruit drink was served as alcohol is prohibited on domestic flights.

As soon as the passengers fastened their seat belts, the TV screens came alive with Mallya addressing the passengers: 'Welcome aboard Kingfisher Airlines. From the day we have started flying, I have tried to create the finest experience for you, and bring back the element of style in travel. Each member of your cabin crew has been hand-picked by me and I have instructed them to treat you as a guest in my own home. In case you have any complaints, please write to me at . . .'

By the time the aircraft with the IATA airline code name IT (something which Mallya boasted of because the airline was based out of the IT capital of the country, Bangalore) landed, Mallya was already famous. The word had gone around that the airline's service quality was top-class, never experienced before in the sector.

'Have you been on Kingfisher?' became a conversation starter in board meetings. Was this the kind of respect which Mallya always aspired for and had he finally got it? The corporate sector was beginning to see him in a new light and with much more respect as they began to realize that his airline was setting new benchmarks in service.

The Rise

During the first few years after its launch, Kingfisher Airlines was the toast of Page 3 as well as the corporate world.

Mallya had become the toast of the nation and everyone wanted to fly Kingfisher. At that point of time, the advice given by some of his own men, including his most trusted lieutenant, Ravi Nedungadi, not to get into the airline venture must have seemed foolishly conservative.

A personal email from one of the top corporate honchos in the country, and there were several of them, was more than effusive in its praise for the airline: 'Whenever I travel in your airline, it makes me feel like a winner. I have asked my senior officials to travel only by your airline. I want the seats to be booked for an entire year.'

On another occasion, a vice president of a big corporate group who was an invitee to aircraft manufacturer Airbus Industrie's showpiece A380's demonstration flight in India, managed to get close to Mallya who was nursing a drink in the aircraft's first-floor lounge. 'Mr Mallya, yesterday your folks didn't carry my bag, you know. Why don't you instruct your staff . . .' The standard of service had been set extremely high and passengers were getting used to being treated spectacularly.

Other airlines just couldn't match up with that kind of service.

Airbus Industrie had flown down the A380, the world's biggest commercial aircraft, to Mumbai in 2007 after Mallya had placed orders for ten of these planes, five on firm sale and the rest on option.

The A380, which costs between $275 million and $400 million for each of the aircraft, was introduced for commercial operations in 2007. It can carry between 525 and 850 passengers depending on the seat configuration.

Meanwhile, what Mallya found in his mailbox regularly was not a list of complaints but accolades for his airline. One such passenger was Tom Peters, celebrated author of the bestselling management book *In Search of Excellence*. In his testimonial to the airline, Peters wrote: 'I've called it [airline's service quality] the ultimate oxymoron for years and years and then more years. Well, that was before I met Kingfisher Air on a roundtrip to Mumbai last week. First there were the "butlers," I guess you'd call them, that carried our bags on and off the plane for those of us lucky enough to be in business class. Courtesy piled upon courtesy, all at a decent price—the food was grand. (Though, truth be known, I think almost all Indian food, as prepared in India, is pretty grand.) But it was that last touch.

'As we neared the beginning of our descent, the flight attendant in biz class walked down the aisle asking us if we'd like her to clean our glasses.

'Holy shit!'

Mallya had left no stone unturned to make the airline the best in its class. He was also looking at increasing the size of the fleet (the A320 family of aircraft) to twelve aircraft by January 2006. The A320 family has been the fastest selling jet airliner in the world since beginning service in 1988. It is a direct competitor to Boeing's 737 family of aircrafts. The narrow-bodied A320 is quite popular among the airlines for its fuel efficiency, competitive pricing as well as for its preferred by domestic operators as it is extremely fuel efficient and has the right capacity for domestic operations. With a single-class seating arrangement, it can accommodate between 150 and 180 passengers and has a sticker price of $88 million. Over 5000 of such aircraft had been sold till July 2012. In the very first year of the launch of the airline, Kingfisher had placed an order for another thirty new A320s worth a total of $1.9 billion. For the uninitiated, it might seem an extremely high amount to pay for but aircraft manufacturers offer what is commonly known as a lease-cum-buy-back arrangement to fund the purchase. This is arranged either through the International Lease Finance Corporation which funds purchase of Airbus aircraft while GE Commercial Aviation Services (GECAS) does it for Boeing.

This is how the lease-cum-buyback arrangement works: the leasing company buys the aircraft on behalf of the airline from the manufacturer. In turn, it leases back the aircraft to the airline on a monthly fee. At the end of the lease period, the aircraft is released by the leasing company to the airline. However, for an airline to make money out of each aircraft, it needs to earn more than the leasing fee it is charged.

Because of such easy terms, Mallya was able to place bigger orders for aircraft purchase.

To deliver the kind of service which would be the envy of most airlines in the country, Mallya had roped in his old buddy, Parvez Damania, former owner of Damania Airways which he had sold to the Chennai-based food-to-wind-power group NEPC.

While many might credit Mallya with introducing service on par with international standards on domestic flights, the credit for being the first to do so should in fact go to Damania who introduced world-class service on his domestic flights.

Parvez and his brother Vispi Damania used to run a hatchery and were regulars in Bombay's Page 3 circles. Together, they floated an airline in 1992 which was perhaps the first to treat its passengers as guests. They were motivated to launch an airline partly because of Madhavrao Scindia, titular head of the royal family of Gwalior and the then Union aviation minister.

During his tenure, Scindia, considered an aspirant for the prime minister's job, decided to introduce the Open Skies policy and throw open aviation to the private sector. The obsolete Air Corporation Act, 1953, was suitably modified to allow private players to initially run air-taxi services and, depending on how successfully they operated them, they would be considered eligible to apply for a licence to run a full-fledged airline.

Some of those who decided to take advantage of

the new policy were ModiLuft, Jet Airways, East-West Airlines and later, Damania Airways. In 1990, the first year of operations of these airlines, the private air-taxi operators carried about 20,000 passengers and, in the next five years, the number had grown to about 5 million, eating into the market share of the state-run Indian Airlines, which had fallen to about 55 per cent.

The Damanias realized that it was not enough to carry passengers from one city to another but to sustain their airline they had to offer better service to the passengers.

Everything that one associated with Kingfisher Airlines, like clean interiors in the aircraft, high-quality ground handling service, courteous staff and fine cutlery on board, was first initiated by Damania Airways. Not only that—the passengers were even offered liquor on board, a first on a domestic airline though the practice was discontinued after stiff opposition from the Hindu nationalist parties.

Damania Airways' popularity soared rapidly. Two years after getting the air-taxi licence, Damania's as well as those of eight others received scheduled domestic airline status.

But with rising aviation turbine fuel prices and

airport taxes, survival was becoming a problem for these airlines. In 1995, the two brothers decided to get rid of their loss-making Damania Airways and sold it off to NEPC.

But NEPC which ran its own regional airline also did not survive for long. Its owner, Ravi Prakash Khemka, whose business interest included operating a 75 MW windmill in south India, was also not able to run the airline profitably and he too exited the business a few years later.

But Damania was back in the airline business soon when he was made a director with Sahara Airlines in 2000. Here, he unleashed the first airfare war among the airlines by drastically reducing Sahara's ticket prices. Other airlines, including Indian Airlines, had no other option but to follow suit. However, due to differences with the management, Damania had to leave Sahara Airways a year later. But it wasn't difficult for Damania to land another job immediately and this time with Kingfisher Airways as an adviser to and director of the airline in 2005.

But his association with the airline was also short lived even though he was able to replicate the same service levels he had introduced in Damania Airways.

Within a year, Damania, along with his brother, Vispi, who was in charge of commercial operations of the airline, quit Kingfisher to pursue their own interests. The Damania's quick exits from each of the airline they worked for did lead to rumours about their differences with the management regarding their style of working. The Damanias have since their latest exit kept a low profile.

This was also one of the first high-profile exits that Kingfisher Airlines witnessed within one year of beginning its operations.

The Fall

'You know, I still remember the compliment you showered on me about my red dress. You said how on earth I could guess the airline's uniform. Oh, that was so cute of you, Vijay.'

The thirty-something former model, a B-lister with make-up which bravely tried to camouflage her age, had managed to get close to her former boss, Vijay Mallya, at a party being hosted by a common friend in an upscale restaurant in Bombay.

The out-of-work siren wasn't done yet. After Mallya had managed to plaster a smile on his face in response to her remark, she went on: 'But, Vijay, the uniform must have changed now, isn't it?' She whispered within his earshot something that sounded like 'dress of mourning'. A usually sharp and quick on the uptake Mallya wasn't going to let that pass easily. But before he could say anything, she had vanished.

This particular piece of gossip came from one of the several Page 3 regulars at Mallya's parties.

One doesn't know whether such a conversation actually took place, but what was true was that this kind of gossip was doing the rounds more frequently, now that Mallya's Kingfisher Airlines was floundering, just three years after the launch.

Mallya could have never imagined that his dream project, 'one of the most important projects in my career', as he described it during the pre-launch conference of the airline, would turn out to be a fiasco. At one of the meetings with the pilots he had just about managed to keep his respect intact.

2010. Kingfisher House, Bombay. The pilots had chosen as their leader someone who happened to be the most vocal among them. He had a sheaf of papers containing a long list of complaints. When those assembled in the room started getting restive, Captain Surjeet replied with a weak smile, 'He is

119

always late.' It was a lame explanation. A UB Group executive tried to keep them in good spirits. 'Dr Mallya told us that we should serve our own Whyte & Mackay's single malt Isle of Jura to everyone.' (UB Group's public relations insist that Mallya should always be referred to as 'Dr Mallya'.) Half of those assembled there weren't interested because they had to fly the next day. The official realized that he had enacted this scene several times for several years now. Except of course on one occasion when his boss turned up right on time for a meeting, causing the official much embarrassment. But why was Mallya habitually late even for some extremely crucial meetings? According to some of his close associates, it could be attributed to his immense ego as there can be no other explanation for being perennially late.

It was nearly midnight when Mallya finally arrived. His presence was electrifying as always. The din created by the chatter among the pilots suddenly evaporated. Those who had decided to confront him with a barrage of demands turned silent in his presence.

'Good evening, sir,' an unnamed pilot, mustering up enough courage, greeted him.

'Sorry, captains, I have been making you wait. But don't take it out on the poor passengers

tomorrow morning for my folly,' Mallya said to no one in particular.

'We had a good drink, sir. Isle of Jura was a class act.' Everyone joined in chorus in praising the drink.

'You know when I bought it for $1.2 billion, everyone said you paid a lot, buddy. But we are no fools. We have already started making money on it,' Mallya said it with a growl followed by a smile, something only he could manage to do.

The assembled pilots nodded together. After all, $1.2 billion wasn't something to be scoffed at.

Mallya could sense that resistance among the pilots was already evaporating. 'So, guys,' he broke off and looked at that lone United Breweries executive, and asked, 'can the dinner be served, please?'

The executive was quick to reply: 'Sir, it is waiting to be served in the next room.'

Mallya walked towards the room, draping his arm around one of the pilots who had managed to get close to him.

Sanjay Aggarwal, the chief executive officer (CEO) of the airline who had accompanied him for the meeting, whispered something in Mallya's ear just as he sat down at the head of the dinner table. Mallya nodded with an amused look on his face. What Aggarwal said may have been very important but Mallya made it look as if it was nothing out of the ordinary. He knew that several pairs of eyes were riveted on his face. Every expression on his face was being analysed by the people at the table with him.

Mallya knew the issues and was worried. One of the banks which had lent funds to him was putting up resistance. His CFO, A. Raghunathan, had done the rounds of that particular bank several times and met the officials, but he had not been able to persuade them to release more funds. This had resulted in a very uncomfortable situation with the salaries being delayed by as many as two months.

It wasn't just the salaries. Oil companies had put the airline on a cash-and-carry basis which meant that they would refuel the aircraft if the money (in cash) for it was paid upfront. There were occasions when the airline officials just didn't have enough cash to pay for the fuel. Services of some of the aircraft had to be suspended suddenly because of that and the ground staff was forced to find seats for its passengers in other airlines. The caterers who supplied meals during the flight were no longer in the mood to oblige because of unpaid bills. They supplied fewer food packets, which meant that not all the passengers got meals, especially during late-evening flights. On some occasions, the passengers had demanded that the pilot give them an explanation in person. The air hostesses were trying their best to manage the situation. On some occasions, they would deliberately delay serving the meals so that not all passengers got them.

Mallya was aware of all that. Every time a flight took off or landed, he would get an SMS about the exact time it departed or arrived.

Mallya finally spoke after a rather long pause: 'You might be interested to know that all the salaries will be paid on time from next month.'

Mallya had deliberately left out raising the issue of arrears. But a pilot keen to get Mallya's reaction on arrears, asked: 'Sir, does it mean we will get our arrears too?'

'What do you think we are?' Mallya growled at him. It made the pilot shrink and the others assembled there gave him a look which suggested that he had in fact insulted the chairman by asking such a question.

The question remained unanswered. Everyone went home from that meeting feeling happy.

The PR machinery worked overtime to 'leak' the news to every aviation correspondent that the airline was all set to clear its dues to every debtor in town.

When some of the journalists asked if the airline had received a fresh infusion of funds, the corporate communication manager said in a hushed tone: 'Why don't you make your own assessment?' That was tip enough for a few TV channels and newspapers to speculate that some unnamed corporate house had emerged as the airline's white knight.

It was pretty obvious that the airline was trying to buy time. When the airline didn't have enough cash to settle the dues of the oil companies, how could it have cash left to pay salaries to its employees? Some of the oil companies dragged the airline to court, asking the promoters to settle their dues. In one such case, a judge is believed to have asked the lawyer representing the airline what its reason was for non-payment of dues to the oil company when it had enough money to own a cricket team. (Mallya owns the Bangalore-based Royal Challengers which plays in the Indian Premier League.)

It left the lawyer red-faced, but he had no explanations to offer the learned judge about Mallya's expensive lifestyle.

Meanwhile, the pilots who had been promised salaries on time hardly got to see any money even after several months.

Then a new problem hit the airline and it became apparent that it had no money to pay anyone. Kingfisher Airlines had issued a cheque of Rs 200 crore to Hindustan Petroleum Corporation Ltd, a state-owned oil marketing company, as payment for dues. When the cheque was deposited, however, it bounced. Earlier, Mallya, a member in the Rajya Sabha, had pulled enough strings within the government to get the oil companies to stagger the payment over a period of six months. Despite that, his airline was unable to keep up to the schedule and kept defaulting.

Over time this became a norm. Most of the cheques issued by the airline started bouncing. The GMR-owned Delhi International Airport didn't think twice before dragging the airline to court after a cheque for Rs 3 crore bounced. The losses continued to mount. In fact, the airline has never made a profit since it began operations in 2005.

Mallya's claim that high oil prices had crippled the airline's operations found no takers as he had not paid the oil companies at all. Hence the issue of rising oil prices was not at all relevant.

In a presentation made to the investors soon after it began operations, the airline had claimed that it would break even by 2008–09. It had also said that, by 2012, it would have its own Kingfisher train called the King Express and a cruise liner called *King Kruise*. The business plan was iron-clad—the UB Group would rule the skies, land and sea within a decade. It was a bit of a mystery that when the business plan for Kingfisher Airlines was being prepared, volatile oil prices, a constant since airlines started using it for transport, was never taken into consideration.

The airline had taken off quite well initially. In 2005, its market share was a mere 15 per cent while that of the leader, Jet Airways, was 30 per cent. By 2007, Kingfisher's market share had jumped to 30 per cent following the merger with the low-cost Air Deccan.

Mallya's ambitions kept soaring; he wanted to make a mark in the international market. During his presentation to the investors, he declared that his airline would compete with the likes of Singapore Airlines and Cathay Pacific within five years. But what prevented him from doing so was a clause in civil aviation norms that stated that no domestic airline could fly international routes unless it completed five full years of domestic operations.

(The Union government now plans to do away with the clause so as to give more freedom to domestic airlines to fly international routes as soon as they start their service.)

One way Mallya could short circuit that clause was by acquiring an airline which already had the eligibility to fly international routes. The only airline, apart from Jet Airways, which fulfilled the norms for flying foreign routes at that time was Air Deccan, run by Captain G.R. Gopinath. Air Deccan was part of the listed entity, Deccan Aviation. As it turned out, Mallya had more than one reason to acquire the airline.

Captain Gopinath was a rising star in the airline industry. He had pulled off a mega deal with Airbus by ordering sixty A320s, worth Rs 12,000, crore when his total bank balance was less than Rs 1 crore. His low-cost model which allowed passengers to fly at less than half the fare full-service carriers charged had shaken the entire industry leading to a situation where competitors were forced to carve out new airlines out of their existing ones just to compete with his model. Air Deccan's Re 1 ticket which could be bought through an online booking process had passengers thronging to his airline.

The Re 1 ticket of course was not what one paid to fly on Air Deccan. It came with airport taxes, all of which added up to Rs 222. But getting one was more difficult than building an airline. People logged on at midnight—at the exact moment a chunk of the tickets were put on sale for Re 1. There was a mad scramble for booking the ticket and funnily it could even be to places which one never intended to go. Such traffic to the Air Deccan website resulted in the company's server crashing several times.

But Captain Gopinath received huge publicity for such gimmicks. In the end this offer turned out to be nothing more than a gimmick because those who were able to get the Re 1 ticket were not exactly the people it was meant for—those who couldn't afford to fly, especially the poor farmers or a schoolteacher in a village. But these people had no easy access to the Internet and hence could not even dream of being able to get the ticket.

The airline also floated Rs 500 tickets which again received a huge response. Because of these offers, Captain Gopinath had turned into a bit of a demigod. He was the saviour of a vast number of people who always wanted to fly abroad but could never do so because of the prohibitive cost of tickets.

On its part, the government could have seized the opportunity provided by Air Deccan and brought down the taxes for lesser priced tickets. However, in spite of the huge demand for air travel, the government continues to impose heavy taxes on airline tickets as well as aviation turbine fuel.

Even as Captain Gopinath's popularity soared, his competitors started feeling the heat as they felt that his airline was becoming a menace because of its disruptive ideas. Captain Gopinath's airline kept ordering more aircraft because it seemed almost everyone in the country wanted to fly Air Deccan.

At one point of time, Captain Gopinath almost seemed unstoppable. The market share of his airline had climbed to 21.2 per cent by July 2006, surpassing the state-owned Indian Airlines. In a statement to the press, Captain Gopinath said the airline had placed orders for 96 more aircraft to be delivered over a period of 96 months.

But such low-priced tickets and flying to previously untapped destinations was costing the airline a lot of money. Aviation turbine fuel prices kept climbing and the state governments which should have been happy with the airline for getting air connections to their cities were in no mood to reduce taxes.

But Mallya and his counterpart in Jet, Naresh Goyal, were getting really worried. Captain Gopinath's statements to the press would read something like this: 'An air ticket for Re 1 plus taxes was our promise to the Indians and every release of a new set of tickets brings us closer to the dream of empowering every Indian to fly.' But it was a clever move. Captain Gopinath was trying to break the monopoly of the bigger players and more or less divert all the passenger traffic to his airline: Who wouldn't want to fly cheap?

Legacy carriers like Jet Airways were finding it difficult to match Air Deccan's prices. Air Deccan had about 70 employees per aircraft whereas Jet had 160 and Kingfisher 125.

So, what was the best way to tackle the problem called Deccan Aviation? One way out was to buy Deccan Aviation, the promoter of Air Deccan itself. Jet couldn't afford to buy another airline after taking over Sahara as it had overleveraged itself. Another, was to start an all-out fare war. The latter, some of Mallya's advisers cautioned him, was not a prudent thing to do.

Therefore, Mallya, in his infinite wisdom, decided that it would be better to buy out Deccan Aviation itself. But it meant paying out a substantial amount of money. Could the UB Group afford to do that at a time when Kingfisher Airlines was still posting losses? But the merger between the two could create one of the largest airlines in the country and as a bonus allow Kingfisher to fly international routes.

Around the same time, Captain Gopinath's dream run was coming to a screeching halt. By December 2006, the airline's parent company, Deccan Aviation, had posted losses of Rs 341 crore on a total income of Rs 1352 crore.

As if the losses weren't enough, Captain Gopinath's decision to buy reservation software from a little-known company called Interglobe Technologies proved to be a huge blunder. The software was not robust enough to handle the kind of traffic which a low-cost airline normally gets. Eventually, it simply crashed, causing mayhem in every booking counter of the airline across the country.

Air Deccan could never recover after that and Captain Gopinath had no other option but to put his airline on the block. But when Mallya formally declared his interest in the airline, Captain Gopinath felt that a merger between a full-service carrier and a low-cost one wouldn't work. 'Mallya is from Venus and I am from Mars and hence a merger between the two airlines is just not possible.'

A year before Kingfisher Airlines acquired Deccan, Captain Gopinath invited the liquor baron to his airline's anniversary celebrations in Bangalore. One doesn't know whether Captain Gopinath was trying to be dramatic or politically correct when he suddenly got up from his seat and invited Mallya to share the dais with him.

Mallya was amused and sportingly took up the offer. Both hugged each other and spoke a few words in their mother tongue, Kannada. At that time, Mallya's airline was still languishing in fourth place in the pecking order but Air Deccan was the number two domestic carrier, next only to Jet Airways.

Mallya used the occasion to declare to the audience that his airline too would one day become the largest in the country and added for good measure that the company would start international operations soon.

Even though Captain Gopinath was reluctant to meet Mallya to hold talks with him over the acquisition of Air Deccan, he was persuaded to do so by a former Karnataka minister who was close to the liquor baron. The men met at Mallya's residence.

The meeting, according to Captain Gopinath, went off well and he was also quite impressed with Mallya's knowledge about the airline industry.

But around the same time, Captain Gopinath was negotiating with Anil Ambani, head of the Anil Dhirubhai Ambani Group (ADAG) to sell his airline. The talks between the two kept dragging for a long time even as Mallya kept pressuring Captain Gopinath to sell the airline to him.

Realizing that his talks with Ambani may not eventually lead to any deal, he opened up negotiations with Mallya. Very soon, a deal was struck between the two. As per the deal, Mallya would pay Captain Gopinath Rs 155 per share to buy 26 per cent stake in the airline's parent, Deccan Aviation. This would trigger off an open offer to buy another 20 per cent from the public. The total outgo to acquire 46 per cent stake in the airline would work out to Rs 1000 crore, including Rs 550 crore for the initial 26 per cent stake.

Once Kingfisher Airlines had picked up 46 per cent stake, a reverse merger with the listed Deccan Aviation was carried out. This way, the unlisted Kingfisher Airlines became a listed company in the Bombay Stock Exchange.

Captain Gopinath told a reporter later that what impressed him about Mallya was how badly he wanted the airline and how swiftly he had moved to bag the deal. When the same reporter asked him whether that meant the deal had been made without any due diligence or checking the balance sheet, Captain Gopinath replied that it was true that during the negotiations, neither Mallya nor his officials ever asked to examine the books. They took Captain Gopinath's assurances at face value because they were eager to go through with the deal.

Curiously, very few analysts raised this issue in their investor reports at that time. At the time of the deal, Air Deccan was twice the size of Kingfisher Airlines in terms of routes, fleet size and revenues.

By early 2008, the combined entity had a market share of 33 per cent—a third of which was Kingfisher Airlines'. The total fleet strength was seventy-one aircraft connecting a total of seventy destinations, making it the largest airline in the country. Kingfisher Airlines launched its first international flight, a Bangalore–London–Bangalore route, and later followed it up with a flight to Sri Lanka. The international operations received extremely good reviews and the airline bagged several awards. Mallya, it seemed, had finally got rid of the 'liquor baron' tag. He was now being seen as the king of the skies.

Once Mallya took control of Air Deccan, his actual intentions surfaced when, within months of acquiring Air Deccan, he went about dismantling whatever the airline stood for.

He first changed the name of the airline to Simplifly Deccan, which simply killed the Air Deccan brand in one stroke. The rebranding exercise involving massive publicity was carried out at a huge cost. Then he took away the Re 1 ticket offer, which had defined whatever Air Deccan stood for.

In his memoirs, *Simply Fly*, Captain Gopinath writes that he could do nothing except stand there and see his dream being torn apart by a man who had promised him before taking over his airline that he would look after it like a baby.

The next to go was the 'Simplifly Deccan' name itself, and the airline was renamed Kingfisher Red. The name change was carried out based on a survey which said that the brand Deccan stood for low cost and hence the management could not raise fares even if it was suffering losses. It sounded quite illogical, but with Mallya in control, everything seemed possible.

Mallya also altered the pricing structure of the airline completely by getting rid of the early bird fares. On several routes, the Air Deccan service was stopped and slowly Kingfisher Airlines flights started taking precedence over those of Air Deccan and now Kingfisher Red. The first consequence of this action which Mallya was to regret later and perhaps was one of the reasons for bringing the airline down as well was that customers started migrating to other low-cost airlines like IndiGo and SpiceJet.

By trying to 'kill' Air Deccan, Mallya had unwittingly started to finish off Kingfisher Airlines itself.

Even as Mallya was dismantling Air Deccan and Captain Gopinath's dream, there was enough turbulence inside Kingfisher Airlines itself. Initially, the money to fund the airline had come from several companies in the UB Group itself. The group also diverted excess staff to the airline as well as recruited some of the top officials from Jet Airways and Sahara.

By 2006, Kingfisher had the full team in place and a year later, SAP AG's enterprise resource planning software, perhaps the costliest such product in the market, was introduced into the system to keep tabs on inventories. With the staff in place, systems on stream, and the country's largest fleet, it seemed just a matter of time before Kingfisher Airlines became the best-run airline in the country.

Unfortunately, it didn't turn out like that. Having everything in place was one issue, the other and more important one was the implementation of Mallya's vision. As a leader, he had provided almost everything the board and the top management could ask for. He had worked hard, spent big dollars, hired the best people and given unlimited funds to his managers, but what was missing was a hands-on person from the industry to run the airline. Almost till the end of 2010, the airline did not have a CEO.

According to insiders, every vice president in the company started acting as if he ran the airline. An ever-busy Mallya just didn't have enough time to devote to the running of the airline. The fact that he hand-picked air hostesses and was always available for customers are just not good enough qualities to operate an airline. It needs a full-time, dedicated CEO, who not only implements the vision of the company but also keeps the herd together and ensures that the day-to-day operations run smoothly.

Kingfisher Airlines consisted of employees who were transferred from the UB Group companies and those who were directly recruited for the airline and had the required experience.

During the initial days, Mallya threw parties in star hotels for the staff, met their families and kept everyone happy. His officials would freely poach from other airlines, doling out double the salaries to new recruits. Unfortunately, not much thought went into such recruitments and it seemed that poaching employees from other airlines was more important than getting the right ones. The joke going around those days was that Jet would let go all those whom it didn't want to retain and kept feeding rumours to the media that Kingfisher had poached some key executives from the airline.

Kingfisher chose to hire executives from Jet for its sales and revenue team as it already had a large number of pilots with half of them coming from other airlines. When the two airlines were competitors, both Air Deccan and Kingfisher Airlines had signed a non-poaching agreement, but as it turned out, the agreement remained on paper.

In order to meet the huge expenses which the airline incurred for paying high salaries and building swanky offices, Mallya had started borrowing from several banks (including the government-owned

State Bank of India), some of which extended the loan without adequate collateral. It looked as if some of the banks had extended loan to the airline based on Mallya's popularity and charisma rather than the real worth of the airline.

When the airline started defaulting on repayment, some of the banks had very little as collateral to fall back upon. The only thing they could do was to have their outstanding loans converted to shares in the airline. But when the stocks sank, hitting new lows every day, all they ended up with was a piece of paper. But more on that later.

Initially, the loans were given in small tranches, about a few hundred crores once in six months for which some of the group companies of United Breweries would stand guarantee. Later, shares of the group companies like United Spirits and UB Holdings began to be pledged to get additional loans.

It increasingly began to look as if Mallya was wrongly advised on launching an airline. Unlike the liquor industry, margins from the airline industry are as low as 3 per cent and hence it is extremely important to run a tight ship.

Hence cost control is extremely essential. Almost everything, right from buying stationery to recruiting employees, has to be done with care and caution. Captain Gopinath was more than careful while spending money and could be a very hard bargainer even if it meant risking losing out on a big deal.

According to at least one employee, Captain Gopinath had once directed the sales staff to travel by bus for sales calls. A few of them objected, stating that if they kept waiting for the bus, they would start losing out on bagging corporate accounts.

On another occasion, one of the top executives is believed to have told a journalist that the airline was toying with the idea of removing one of the two washrooms in the aircraft to make way for a few more seats which would earn them more revenues. The journalist went back shaking his head, repelled at the thought of something like that being actually implemented on Air Deccan flights.

Mallya, though, was the exact opposite. He hired or poached employees from other airlines and gave them hikes which were as high as 75 per cent. He was either being very generous or simply foolish when he decided not to fire even a single employee from Deccan Aviation after he acquired the airline. The move earned him the eternal gratitude of the staff, but the airline itself was burdened with excess manpower which meant the salary bills went through the roof.

The airline also became top heavy because of not rightsizing the staff. At one time, there were about forty officials working as either general managers or vice presidents and drawing salaries amounting to lakhs per month.

Some of the employees who were interviewed for this book but did not want to be quoted said that everything the airline implemented bordered on extravagance.

For example, if a passenger turned up late at the check-in counter, he would not be turned away. Instead, one of the counter staff would buy him a ticket in another airline. All airlines work on dynamic pricing as far as tickets are concerned. Hence, tickets bought just before the departure of an aircraft are the most expensive. For example, if a passenger booked a ticket in advance, he would be able to buy it for as low as Rs 4000 and if the same ticket was bought on the day of the departure, it could cost as high as Rs 12,000.

No wonder passengers loved the airline and still want to fly Kingfisher. It is another matter that a revived Kingfisher might turn out to be a different experience altogether, because in case the airline does get back on its wings, Mallya cannot afford such largesse.

On other occasions, in case a flight was delayed and some passengers protested, they would be taken to the nearest five-star hotel and served unlimited quantities of snacks and beer. A pint of beer at a five-star costs as much as Rs 250, but the airline front desk at the airports would grudgingly foot the bill. Some passengers would point out that as Mallya was a liquor baron, the least the airline could do was to serve them liquor whenever their flights got delayed. It was an argument that the gound staff could have easily countered but for reasons best known to them, the 'aggrieved' passengers were accorded the royal treatment.

Even though he was never on time for any of his meetings, Mallya ensured that the flights took off on time. The ground staff had to send him a message the moment a flight took off and as soon as it landed in another airport. Even a five-minute delay was not tolerated and those responsible for the delay got an earful from Mallya himself.

It was actually a strange place to work for. There was hardly any accountability as far as spending money was concerned. At one point, it seemed that money was leaking out from every level and there were no checks and balances in place to run a tight ship.

'We weren't sure if the money was being utilized properly,' an employee working with the finance department had once revealed to a journalist. For example, most of the newspapers and magazines, including international ones, bought for the passengers were left at the warehouse instead of being loaded on to the flights, though the bills for them were paid promptly. No survey was carried out to find out what kind of publication the passengers wanted to read in-flight. Some of the publications were bought from the news stands instead of taking long-term subscriptions which would have come at half the cover price.

It took a lot of effort and convincing on the part of the finance department to sell them to old newspaper vendors. But once the clearance was given, the sale of old newspapers and magazines alone fetched a few lakh rupees every month.

The international operations was another story altogether. The first international flight was from Bangalore to London was launched on 3 September

2008 and soon after, the Bangalore–Colombo flight took off. It was assumed that Londoners would find the route attractive enough if they thought of holidaying in south India and in Sri Lanka as well. The flight would also cater to the needs of employees of IT companies based out of the IT capital, Bangalore.

According to the airline consultancy firm Centre for Asia-Pacific Aviation, the level of service on these flights was among the best offered by any international airline.

But what Kingfisher had not taken into consideration was that the introduction of its flight would unleash a price war among airlines. Several foreign airlines started offering attractive lower fares on this route. They were able to do it because they had enough money to burn to fend off the competition. Surprisingly, Kingfisher refused to join the price war, saying that its services were far superior. But it was quite obvious that an airline which was just a few years old and was launching its first international flight did not have enough spare cash to take on the well-entrenched foreign airlines.

Airline pundits will tell you that if you are launching a new service you should either have enough cash in the bank so that you can take on whatever is thrown at you by the competition or offer fares which are the lowest in the industry in the beginning itself. For example, Air Asia offers extremely low fares unmatched by other competing airlines for destinations in South East Asia. If you book tickets months in advance, the fares you get are at least 15–20 per cent lower.

Could Kingfisher follow suit? Passengers, especially those on holiday trips, are extremely cost conscious because they are paying out of their own pockets. They would rather splurge on touring more places than on transport.

Kingfisher tried to stick around rather gamely in the ring for some time at least. But its domestic operations were floundering—something it could ill afford at a time when it was expanding international operations which needed millions of rupees to stabilize. The funds from the banks were drying up and at least one senior official revealed that once the banks closed the tap, Kingfisher started defaulting on payments to everyone.

By late 2008, the first signs of trouble in Mallya's airborne empire started showing. The US-based GECAS filed a complaint with the Indian aviation regulator, the Directorate General of Civil Aviation (DGCA), saying that Kingfisher Airlines had defaulted on rentals for four A320s, and GECAS was seeking to repossess the aircraft.

The complaint was duly received but Mallya wielded such clout in the corridors of power that other than sending a notice and a reminder, no action was taken. A frustrated GECAS then decided to drag the airline to court. It filed a case against the airline in the Karnataka High Court. But the airline managed to secure an 'ad interim' relief from the court to prevent repossession.

However, this piece of news was enough for intrepid reporters to begin sniffing around. Analysts tracking the company's stocks smelt a rat and started going through the balance sheet of the airline with a fine-tooth comb.

The combined entity was bleeding. Deccan Aviation's loss prior to the merger added to the losses incurred by Kingfisher Airlines was a whopping Rs 2000 crore. It was becoming obvious that, at least in this case, two negatives did not make a positive.

Unable to sustain large-scale operations because of its continued losses, the airline announced that it had deferred deliveries of thirty-two A320 family aircraft by two years to 2010–12 and planned to return fourteen narrow-bodied leased aircraft to downsize its operations.

More trouble was mounting for the airline and so were the losses. In September 2011, the airline management stopped the operations of Kingfisher Red, stating that it no longer believed in the low-cost airline model. By then, the airline's market share had sunk to a new low of 14 per cent and the airline had dropped to the fifth position in the pecking order while passenger traffic grew 17.1 per cent. Jet Airways' share, on the other hand, was 27.1 per cent and it topped the chart.

Meanwhile, the passenger feedback book started looking very different. The prestigious London-based industry consultancy company Skytrax which had awarded the airline a five-star rating decided not to rank the airline anymore. On its website, a passenger from Australia, Sonia Mitchells, wrote: 'Hong Kong to Delhi. Check-in staff were rude and ignorant, we were left at the service desks for almost 30 mins unattended. The inflight entertainment did not work for the middle of the cabin. The toilets were not kept clean. We were travelling with a 10 month infant and there was no bassinet or seatbelt provided. Seats were uncomfortable and 5 out of the 6 seats we booked had some type of fault in it (cup holder broken, remote broken etc).'

Another passenger, Patrick Brompton from the UK, wrote: '. . . With regret, I would not book Kingfisher again as it is now an unreliable operator, delaying and cancelling our internal flight, maintaining its intercontinental flights but for how long?'

In September 2009, international operations to London and Colombo were withdrawn. The airline claimed that it was trying to ensure optimal and efficient fleet operations. By April 2012, all international flights were cancelled, the airline stating that credit restrictions from banks had made it increasingly difficult for it to operate these flights. Also, the International Air Transport Association (IATA), which acts as a clearing house between businesses, suspended the billing facility to the airline, and the leasing companies started recalling the aircraft one after another.

For an airline which had sunk about Rs 1000 crore to buy Deccan Aviation so that it could fast-track its way to obtaining the licence to fly international routes, the suspension by IATA came as a rude shock. Almost everything that Mallya wanted to do with his airline had come to nought. His ambition to become another Richard Branson (at one time he had famously claimed that Branson was in fact the Vijay Mallya of the UK) had turned out to be a big flop.

Those pilots who decided to stay back launched an agitation to get their dues but it was clear that the management wasn't settling any of those; anyone who wanted to leave the company was told to do so. Most of the pilots had joined the airline because of Mallya's charisma. But their patience began wearing thin when they realized that the airline couldn't be bothered to take care of even their basic needs, and their charismatic leader was never around to talk to them.

Home loan EMIs remained unpaid for several months and school fees of the employees' children kept getting deferred. On one occasion, according to a newspaper report, when two of their junior colleagues were thrown out by their landlords in the middle of the night for not paying their rents, some of the pilots managed to get some money and paid the rent on their behalf. In times of such crisis, the management was just not forthcoming with any help.

The last straw was when it was revealed in the 2011–12 annual report of the airline that CEO Sanjay Agarwal's salary for 2011–12 had been doubled to Rs 4.01 crore. This, at a time when the pilots, air hostesses and other staff had not been paid for months.

The lenders who had waited patiently enough for the airline to turn around didn't see much hope. A consortium of banks led by the State Bank of India had ended up with a huge exposure in terms of loans extended to the airline industry, and in the case of Kingfisher Airlines, it was the highest. But the country's central bank, the Reserve Bank of India, based on requests from the airline industry and under pressure from the Centre, agreed to allow a one-time debt recast for all the airlines in September 2010.

Debt recasts are usually offered to bail a company out of its financial mess. In the case of Kingfisher Airlines, a State Bank of India-led consortium of thirteen banks agreed to convert part of the debt— Rs 1300 crore—into equity through preference shares by acquiring the airline's shares at Rs 63 per equity share. This meant that the banks ended up holding 23.2 per cent stake in the airline. Other terms were softened while the interest rate was lowered to 11 per cent and the period of repayment stretched to nine years.

The news of the debt recast was met with stinging criticism from some of the country's most respected financial analysts. A Canadian investment research firm, Veritas, termed the recast as a giant, collective swindle of public money. 'We do not believe that KFA's [Kingfisher Airlines's] antics would have found any takers in a responsible credit market, and that the airline would have been liquidated by now . . . The banking consortium is now both the owner and a creditor to the airline, thereby complicating an intractable situation further, and jeopardizing its role as a steward of shareholder and depositor capital,' Veritas wrote.

Despite the recast, more problems piled up on Kingfisher Airlines.

In a reply to the Rajya Sabha in December 2011, the Union minister of state for finance, S.S. Palanimanickam, revealed that the airline had not deposited tax deducted at source from employees' salaries into the exchequer. He said that proceedings had been initiated against the airline for recovering the amount and the interest as well. The airline had not just defaulted for one year but for two continuous years. For 2010–11, the liability was Rs 52.82 crore and for 2011–12 it was about Rs 100 crore. In simple terms, the citizens of the country had been robbed of their dues. The airline, as of May 2013, owes the consortium of banks a whopping Rs 7037 crore.

As a result of this, the tax department froze the bank accounts of the airline in February 2012, which in turn caused further delays in paying salaries to the staff. The accounts were unfrozen in April that year so that the airline could pay salaries to the pilots and other staffers. Even after that, the airline paid the employees only a couple of months' salary.

The airline had gone into what looked like a never-ending tailspin. Mallya's image was at its lowest ebb. *Firstpost*, an online newsmagazine, describing the crumbling empire of the liquor baron, wrote: 'Kingfisher is practically over. Mallya is down to his underpants—like many of his calendar models.'

In their report for 2011–12, the auditors of the airline pointed out a major discrepancy in the preparation of the financial statement. They noted that the financial statements were prepared on a 'going concern' basis, even though the airline's net worth had been completely eroded. In other words, the financial statement of the company, which is a barometer of its health, was prepared on the misleading assumption of it being an entity which did not face any threat of closure. Whereas, in fact, the airline's total liabilities were greater than its total assets. The annual report also pointed out that the airline's total losses had more than doubled to Rs 2328 crore in 2011–12, from Rs 1027 crore in the previous year. Its long-term borrowings stood at Rs 5695 crore as on 31 March 2012, and short-term borrowings at Rs 2335 crore at the end of 2011–12, up from Rs 604 crore as on 31 March 2011.

For these loans, Kingfisher Airlines had used as security all its movable assets, trademarks, 'goodwill' of the company, credit cards and other receivables and a mortgage on Kingfisher House.

The banks kept up the pressure on the management of the airline. Whenever the bank officials called for a meeting with Kingfisher Airlines, a few executives from the management would turn up with a presentation making claims about a possible revival in the near future.

But it wasn't of much help. Around the same

time, at an annual general meeting of the airline in Bangalore, Mallya kept losing his cool while answering questions from journalists who had gathered there.

The next day at the AGM of his holding company he claimed that the media had become extremely vindictive. 'I told you that today's newspapers will carry big headlines that Kingfisher shareholders want Mallya out. But all of you know what happened at the AGM yesterday. They were all praising me for my brave efforts to rescue the airline.'

On the previous day, some of the shareholders had in fact raised inconvenient questions to the management asking them the reason for the airline's decline. One angry shareholder told the management that if it could not run the airline properly, then they should resign en masse.

Another shareholder, a vendor of the airline, pleaded with Mallya to return the money the airline owed to him. 'Why don't you give me tickets so that I can sell them to recover the dues?'

Some others were kinder to Mallya, and praised him for being a braveheart. Mallya had ignored the rest of the comments and chosen to highlight only those which praised him at the following day's meeting.

The Good Shepherd School on Residency Road in Bangalore had become a regular venue for the UB Group to conduct its AGMs. Years ago, it used to be Chowdiah Hall, the sprawling auditorium shaped like a violin. The auditorium was named after a famous violinist, Chowdiah. Holding AGMs there was considered prestigious and the public-relations cell of the group made it a point to call every newspaper in the city to attend the meeting. And to thank them for their presence, journalists were handed a goody bag consisting of some products of the UB Group.

But that was when times were really good, long before Mallya had anointed himself the 'king of good times'. Soon after he had taken over the reins of the group, Mallya had started visiting newspaper offices and wooing journalists. Mallya's key officials sought out journalists and spent a large amount of time giving interviews. United Breweries' head Kalyan Ganguly and United Spirits' chief Vijay Rekhi cultivated the media pretty well. Journalists were regularly invited to fashion shows conducted by the group, to derbys and almost every part of the group was open to them.

However, most of it stopped once the airline

started going down. A once-transparent group had become opaque. Mallya was hard to get. The Gangulys and Rekhis had more or less moved out of the circuit while the very affable Ravi Nedungadi, who helped Mallya in some of his acquisitions, had turned silent.

To make matters worse, a financial newspaper quoted Nedungadi as saying he had always been against floating an airline and had tried in vain to dissuade Mallya. Journalists had suddenly become outcasts for the UB Group. 'Journalists are always trying to put us down. They think we have gone bankrupt. I am not going anywhere. My shareholders have benefited a lot,' Mallya thundered during the AGM.

It had now become the norm for Mallya to hold forth against journalists. Some of the shareholders whom journalists later interviewed felt the same. 'He is being unfairly targeted. We have been regularly getting good returns. Then what is the problem?' said a shareholder. It was true. Most of the UB Group shares had performed extremely well in the market giving returns as high as 200–300 per cent.

Soon after Diageo announced its decision to buy into United Spirits, the stocks touched Rs 2000 per share when the open offer itself was priced at

Rs 1440. Kingfisher Airlines' stock which had touched a low of Rs 8 climbed to about Rs 30 and higher.

Meanwhile, the vendor who had raised a din at the shareholders' meeting was intent on getting his due from the airline. He came out of the AGM and held an impromptu press conference giving details of how much the airline owed him and how he had been continuously denied an audience with Mallya. 'I was sent an email by an official promising me Rs 45 lakh due to me. I was also told that Mallya would give me a cheque at the AGM. But he merely asked me to contact the officials again,' said Wing Commander Raghuraman whose company, Adisys Solutions, provided ground support services to the airline.

'I have no confidence in the airline. Mallya keeps saying he will give salaries to his employees but nothing has happened so far. I will exit the day the shares go up even slightly,' he continued.

Not much is known about what happened to Raghuraman or whether he eventually received payments from the airline. But going by the number of cases filed in various Bangalore courts by lenders, it was quite clear that the airline had defaulted several times in clearing the bills of vendors as well as lenders.

Soon after the AGM, some reporters sneaked into the auditorium to meet Mallya.

'What do they want to speak to me about?' asked Mallya when his public-relations executive, Beena Omprakash, conveyed the reporters' request. She had earlier dissuaded the reporters from talking to Mallya but when she saw the reporters wouldn't budge, she was forced to talk to Mallya.

'So, you want to talk to me. How can I help you?' asked a visibly tired Mallya.

'Sir, we wanted to know what you are going to do about the airline. How are you planning to revive it?' asked a rather young CNBC TV18 reporter.

'Who said it is not doing well? You people have already written it off. Your television channel was good to me earlier. Now, you write all sorts of things without verifying anything,' Mallya held forth. The lady reporter remained silent as the billionaire kept up the verbal barrage.

Then came the sudden outburst that caught everyone by surprise: 'You want to take me on. Do it! I have nothing to fear. I will sell off everything. Go to Los Angeles where my son is doing a course in entertainment. [Siddharth had enrolled himself in an acting course.] *What will you do?'*

Mallya was never given to outbursts, at least not publicly. He was always known to be cool. Outside, a swarm of reporters kept pushing the corporate communications team to get Mallya to address them. When he arrived, Mallya repeated what he had told his shareholders: 'We are in talks with an airline.' When a reporter asked him for the name, Mallya shot back: 'Why should I tell you?' and walked away.

A rather intrepid reporter chased him and asked him why his son Siddharth, a director on the board, was not present at the AGM where he was re-elected:

'Dr Mallya, where is Siddharth? He was not present at the AGM.'

'Why do you want to know?' asked Mallya.

'Because he was standing for re-election to the board.'

'How is it important for your newspaper?' Mallya shot back, clearly getting irritated with the reporter's persistence.

'Because it is important for the shareholders . . .'

'Why don't you find something more important for your readers?' Mallya said just as his security men closed out the reporter.

Everyone present there knew that it wasn't the good ol' Mallya any more. Reporters were surprised to find him a bit uncomfortable in answering questions, a rarity hitherto. But then, nobody had asked him difficult questions before this. Reporters generally admired Mallya for his flamboyance, and some of them were in awe of him. But at the bourses, Kingfisher Airlines' stocks rose significantly following Mallya's announcement that he was negotiating with a foreign airline to pick up stake in his airline.

But nothing of that sort happened. It seemed that Mallya was merely making empty promises and there was no foreign airline anywhere on the horizon to even consider an alliance with Kingfisher.

Even the civil aviation ministry's regulator was losing patience with the airline management's promises of paying salaries, clearing dues of the oil companies and repaying bank loans. On 20 October 2012, the regulator finally suspended the airline's licence and a few months later took away its airport-time slots.

Mallya kept making promises stating that he would revive his airline, but in June 2013 he finally admitted to his remaining 2000-odd employees that he did not have the money to pay their salaries.

One may want to agree with Warren Buffet's observation about the airline industry that its demand for capital ever since that first flight has been insatiable—'Investors have poured money into a bottomless pit, attracted by growth when they should have been repelled by it'—which goes to show that it is all the more important for airline promoters to be extremely prudent.

In the case of Kingfisher Airlines, Mallya was short on experience when it came to running an airline. This drawback was compounded by the fact that he assumed that he could run it himself instead of leaving it to professionals. Even if had hired someone from the industry to manage the airline, he would have remained a complete hands-on boss which sometimes can be seen as being a control freak by a CEO. As his airline kept going down, Mallya came up with one excuse after another, blamed almost everyone except himself: it was either the media or the government's policies or the oil prices which were the reasons for his downfall or quite simply his bad luck.

So, what finally led to the fall of Kingfisher Airlines? Was it the ill-fated acquisition of Deccan Aviation's Air Deccan or was it the fact that Mallya wanted to run the airline on lenders' money or was it both? Did he overreach himself?

When he began his airline, Mallya had almost everyone rooting for him. That he squandered away such goodwill clearly shows that he should have appointed a professional CEO to run the airline and distanced himself from the day-to-day operations.

What also alienated him from several well-meaning friends in the corporate sector as well as in political circles was his display of wealth at a time when several hundreds of his employees had not been paid salaries for months together apart from the taxes worth crores that he failed to pay to the government.

During one of his visits to India, Richard Branson, the owner of Virgin Atlantic and Virgin Records, made a pointed remark that display of wealth was never in the best interest of anyone. To which Mallya tweeted back saying that he had learnt his lessons and had realized that the display of wealth, especially in India, was the wrong thing to do.

Ultimately, for all his ambitions, his airline business dealt what was perhaps the heaviest blow to his image, something even his competitors could not do. Not even the Chhabria brothers.

The lenders, meanwhile, have started proceedings against the airline and have so far got the local court to allow a winding-up petition against the group's holding company, UB Holdings. If the court rules in favour of the lenders, the group would have lost its crown and perhaps that would be the beginning of the end of the Mallya empire.

8

The IPL Adventure

The Indian Premier League or the IPL is the single biggest sporting event in India. According to the brand valuation company, American Appraisal, it is currently valued at a whopping $3.2 billion.

But before the IPL came into being, a similar kind of tournament was organized by media moghul Subhash Chandra in 2007. Realizing the enormous potential the game of cricket offered, Chandra decided to start a championship tournament along the lines of the popular English Premier League, which organizes football matches in the UK.

He wasn't just keen on starting a tournament but also wanted to set up a parallel cricket body which could take on the Board of Cricket Control in India (BCCI). He roped in several famous cricketers including former Indian captain Kapil Dev to launch the tournament.

Called the Indian Cricket League (ICL), the tournament which was based on the shortest format of the game, a twenty-over match (T20) between two teams, took off in 2007. However, the BCCI quickly saw through the design behind floating such a venture. As the BCCI itself is a private body, it realized it could not ban another private body. Hence, it decided to come down heavily on cricketers who were taking part in the tournament by banning them from participating in any of the matches conducted by the BCCI.

The ban had immediate repercussions. Several cricketers who were part of the ICL decided to return to the BCCI fold under an amnesty scheme floated for this purpose. Unable to attract even club-class cricketers because of the ban, the ICL folded up in 2009.

However, the tournament itself had fired the imagination of the BCCI which realized that if it did not start a league of its own, there could be several other ICLs in the offing.

Therefore, it decided to have its own tournament and gave the task of starting one such event to its enterprising vice president, Lalit Modi. Son of industrialist K.K. Modi and owner of the $6 billion Modi Enterprises, Modi was known for his excellent organizational skills. Within months, he put together a new tournament called the Indian Premier League (IPL). The IPL too would follow the T20 match format but the teams would be owned by corporate houses who would have to bid to get their teams to play in the tournament. To form a team, the players would offer themselves for bids from the team owners.

The tournament took off in 2008 with participation from eight teams, each of them owned by business tycoons and movie stars.

The format fascinated Mallya who was keen to associate his group with India's most popular sport.

Mallya saw a huge opportunity for the promotion of his brands through the IPL. As no liquor company operating in India can directly advertise its brands; the only way to do it is through surrogate advertising. Therefore, these companies sponsor sporting events under the brand name of their liquor products. In fact, the name given to the UB Group's airline was a brand extension of Kingfisher beer, which became a more popular brand than the mother brand itself.

Mallya managed to win the bid for the Bangalore

team, paying $111.6 million for it—the second highest among all the bids. He named his team after one of his liquor brands—Royal Challengers Bangalore. There were seven other teams in the tournament and while the total base price for the auction was $400 million, it eventually gave the organizers a total of $724 million.

The winners of the auction were declared in January 2008 and the tournament was scheduled to begin in April. Rahul Dravid was named captain of the Royal Challengers and New Zealand legend Martin Crowe was signed on as the coach. Charu Sharma, a cricket commentator and sporting event organizer, was appointed the CEO.

But even before the first few games had been played, Sharma was sacked for 'non-performance' though it was the cricketers who were losing the matches.

Tall and well built, Sharma was well known as a cricket commentator who also organized sporting events across the country. Known for his chatty style of commentary, he had a fan following of his own. Mallya had met Sharma at one of the parties and sounded him out for the CEO's job. 'Would you like to be involved now that we have decided to bid?'

Mallya had asked Sharma. It wasn't exactly an offer he could refuse but Sharma thought that being involved would not take all his time. The IPL was still new and no one knew what kind of a beast it would turn out to be. Sharma decided to take the plunge and accepted Mallya's offer.

The tournament's inaugural match held on 18 April 2008 at the M. Chinnaswamy Stadium was between the Royal Challengers and the Kolkata Knight Riders, the team owned by movie star Shahrukh Khan. The match began at 8 p.m. but within a couple of hours, New Zealand batsman Brendon McCullam, playing for the Kolkata Knight Riders, had completely changed the course of the match by hitting 158 runs in a mere 73 balls.

It was the highest T20 score till then. According to a report in ESPNCricinfo, 'The punch-drunk Bangalore team was in no condition to fight back after that battering, and collapsed limply to 82 to lose by an embarrassing margin of 140 runs, the fourth-largest defeat in this sort of a format.'

By the time the tournament was about to enter its second phase, the Royal Challengers had already lost five matches, including one against the lowly rated King's XI Punjab.

Sharma recalls how he got the sack while he was on his way to the airport to catch a flight to Kolkata.

The car in which Charu Sharma was travelling was about to enter the airport when he received a call from one of the top officials in the UB Group. 'Hi. Where are you?'

'I am about to enter the airport. The next leg of the tournament is to begin the day after. You know it is going to be pretty hectic from tomorrow onwards,' Sharma replied.

'Charu, can you return to the office immediately?'

'Right now?' asked Sharma.

'Yup. Right away.'

'But I am about to board the flight. Can we meet after I return?'

'Well, you see we want you back right now,' the official said, and hung up.

Realizing that something was seriously wrong, Sharma diverted the car back to the UB Group's office. He was ushered in right away into the official's room.

'Hi. Have a seat, Charu,' the official invited. 'Well, you see, how is the tournament going on? All well?'

'You know. We haven't actually done well so

far but there are still seven more matches to go. We expect to do well in those. The boys are just about getting used to the format,' Sharma offered as an explanation for the rather dismal performance of his team.

'Looks like the "boys" in the other teams have got used to the format much earlier. Anyway, let me keep this short. We have decided to let you go,' the official declared.

Sharma was stunned. But known for his quick repartees, he asked: 'Is it because I didn't bat well or bowl?'

'You know how it is. The management feels that it needs to straighten up a few things. Also, we didn't like your interview to that financial daily where you said that it will take some more time for IPL teams to start making profits,' the official offered by way of an explanation.

Sharma was aware that not everyone was happy with that interview. But he still put up a defence. 'Isn't it true? You don't make money immediately. It takes time.' The argument went back and forth until the honcho asked him to put in his papers. Sharma decided against it and asked him to sack him.

'Well, take your time and we will give you another twenty-four hours,' the official replied.

By the time Sharma returned to his residence, just a few kilometres away from the UB Group headquarters, the television channels had already started airing the news that Mallya had sacked his CEO. Sharma called up the official he had met mere hours ago and asked him why the story was appearing in the evening news. He was told that 'it must have leaked somehow'.

'But there was no one else apart from the two of us in the room,' Sharma pointed out.

Sharma realized that silence on his part could be misconstrued. The next day in a statement Sharma said: 'I am not a quitter, especially when the chips are down. The company has every right to hire and fire personnel. For details of why I was summarily dismissed from my duties three hours before I was to board a flight to Kolkata for the next match, please contact representatives of the company.'

The Royal Challengers had earlier issued a statement that Sharma had 'stepped down due to personal reasons'. He was immediately replaced with former test cricketer Brijesh Patel. Curiously, both Patel and Mallya were in opposite camps during the elections for the general body of the Karnataka State Cricket Association, the state wing of the BCCI.

Insiders say that initially Mallya showed a lot of interest in the team but after some time, he left it to the Dravid–Crowe–Sharma combine to run the operations. Mallya would call the CEO once in a while and if both had to meet, he would be told to fly down to Delhi or wherever he was, sometimes as late as 3 a.m. The company's marketing team was put at the IPL team's disposal which made it much easier to get such things done quickly. But to get experienced people to run various parts of the operations was difficult.

The auction for players had turned out to be controversial. 'You may have a list of players you want to pick but it is not necessary you will land up with those whom you want,' explains Sharma. If the team owner wants a certain player desperately, he might actually get him but at a price which would mean that he might not have enough money to pay for the others whom the team needs. The auctions are televised live and one can actually see former players assisting team owners to pick the best of the lot. But by the end of the day, it is clear that no one has got the player he wants. Curiously, some unknown players are bought for enormous amounts of money and those who are expected to make the most end up making far less.

For the Royal Challengers, the accusation was that the team Dravid and Charu Sharma picked was more of a test-playing eleven with the likes of South African Jacques Kallis and Indian test opener Wasim Jaffer, both not exactly known for their exploits in the shorter version of the game. But in reality, the Royal Challengers had a good bowling attack which included Dale Steyn of South Africa and spinner and former Indian captain Anil Kumble. However, neither player was able to make it for the matches due to injuries which proved to be a big handicap for the team. 'It was a bowler-heavy team without the key bowlers,' as a wag put it.

The nature of T20 is such that the outcome of the matches remains undecided until the last ball. But the first Royal Challengers game was a disaster. Mallya, who feeds on publicity, was very disappointed. He obviously didn't take kindly to such a poor show. Questions were raised during office meetings and at parties as well. When the team officials tried to pacify the company top brass, stating that the outcomes of these matches were based on luck or just on one bad over, they were told that the UB Group makes its own luck.

The players were also nudged to attend post-match parties hosted by Mallya. Some of them turned up but those who were too tired gave it a miss, only to be told that their absence was not appreciated. Mallya was under extreme pressure to act and show to the world that he was the man in charge. No amount of explanation was good enough. He eventually acted but as some of the players said later, he ended up making the CEO the scapegoat for the team's bad run. There were cries for Dravid's scalp too but that would probably have been too severe a step.

Sharma was having a bad time too. There were too many things to do and when his father passed away he just about managed to attend the funeral before returning to work the next day. His relatives just couldn't understand how a son could not be there to perform all the rites. But it was not that easy to step aside and let someone else take control of the IPL team. Being the CEO, it was his responsibility to get the team off the ground and see to it that it performed to its potential. While the coach saw to it that the team delivered and played as a cohesive group, it was his job to put together a system which ensured that the team could focus on their job.

Accusations were being traded thick and fast.

Mallya later justified in an interview with NDTV that when he asked the players about their lacklustre performance, he was told that it was because of poor infrastructure and lack of practice. He also said that while he had his own list of players, he had decided to allow Dravid and Sharma to have their say as he believed in their judgment. But Sharma claimed that the task of choosing the players had been left to Dravid and Kumble. Dravid too said that though the players picked for the team were right, it was just one long bad run which was leading to criticism about its composition.

The Royal Challengers subsequently made up for their poor show in later editions of the tournament. What is important to learn from all this is that Indian corporate houses look at owning a sports team differently from those in the West. In the West, tycoons own sports teams not to make money but to make a statement that they have arrived. It is seen as a prestigious thing, something like owning a super luxury car. They are not, as Sharma pointed out, bought to make more money.

Since the controversial beginning of the Royal Challengers, the team has settled down and been the runner-up in two editions of the tournament so far.

But its brand value has eroded considerably. According to one brand valuation company, the Royal Challengers' valuation has dipped nearly 10 per cent to about $40 million with the brand rating going down to 'A minus' from 'A plus'. There have been occasional rumours of Mallya planning to sell off the team but at such low valuations, he might hardly be able to square off his investments in the team.

9

Acquiring Whyte & Mackay

The CEO of the powerful SWA, Gavin Hewitt, kept pacing up and down his office with a worried expression on his face. He couldn't imagine that a Scotch whisky maker from his own backyard was in talks to sell out to an Indian liquor baron. After all, the SWA had mounted a huge campaign, moved the European Union which in turn had petitioned to the World Trade Organization, to stop discriminatory taxes on imported spirits and wines by India.

Not just that, the SWA had refused to recognize whisky made from molasses. This norm had virtually kept Indian liquor makers such as United Spirits from accessing the highly lucrative markets in Europe. The SWA recognizes only grain-based whiskies and anything other than that is considered rum or even juice.

At one point of time, the tax on imported liquor was as high as between 200 per cent and 800 per cent on the sale price, depending upon the type of liquor and which state it was being sold in. It was well known in government circles that the lobby behind the decision to impose such heavy taxes was led by United Spirits which controls over 70 per cent of the industry. Any lowering of the taxes would have immediately impacted the sale of the largest Indian liquor maker.

In such a scenario, Mallya was now all set to buy Whyte & Mackay (earlier known as Kyndal), a bulk Scotch whisky maker with a Scottish pedigree.

Whyte & Mackay's majority owner, Vivian Imerman, was apparently under a lot of pressure from the SWA to choose a buyer from Scotland instead of looking at overseas buyers. (Incidentally, years ago, Whyte & Mackay had a distribution and marketing arrangement for its products with Shaw Wallace.) Imerman and his brother-in-law, Iranian property developer Robert Tchenguiz (who bought the UK-based supermarket group Somerfield, along with others, for slightly over £1 billion in 2005), were the newly crowned takeover tycoons at the turn of the century. Imerman had sold Del Monte to

Italian group Cirio Finanziaria before buying Whyte & Mackay.

Imerman had fought hard to take control of Whyte & Mackay and managed to get full ownership of the company sometime in 2005. He began restructuring the company as soon as he took over. Imerman wanted to position the Scottish company as a global spirits major and hence started reorganizing it, cutting flab and putting the focus on his goal. But midway through the exercise, he either lost steam because too much money was involved or simply lost interest. A year or so later, he was ready to put it on the block.

But Imerman wasn't going to sell the company cheap. The company, with a history of over a century, had about 10 per cent market share globally and a group of investors had paid about £208 million to buy Whyte & Mackay in 2011.

When the company was put on the block, Mallya immediately got wind of it and started making discreet inquiries about its viability. Whyte & Mackay also had reserves of about $200 million of Scotch, apart from owning brands such as Dalmore and Isle of Jura.

For Mallya there were two reasons to own

Whyte & Mackay: He wanted to buy Scotch produced in bulk so that it could be mixed with his company's IMFL products and sold at a higher price. Buying Scotch from the open market can be prohibitively expensive.

The second reason was to get some legitimacy in the world market dominated by players like Diageo and Pernod Ricard. Mallya kept meeting Imerman whenever he visited his second home, London, where his first wife, Sameera, son, Siddharth, and his mother, Lalitha, lived. However, Imerman kept fending off Mallya's overtures but the latter persistently raised the bid.

As some wag said, if Mallya sets his eyes on something, only a world war can stop him from getting it. If he did not win the company or the board he had bid for, it was perhaps because he had a change of mind at the last minute.

Imerman had also confirmed that he was evaluating more than one unsolicited bid but hadn't disclosed the suitors' names. Whyte & Mackay had been valued at about £600 million at that time. Mallya's United Spirits, however, had valued the company at about £475 million.

Talks had begun a few years before the deal was

struck in May 2007. Both the companies were playing the waiting game to perfection. Neither of them had budged from their stated price. Mallya had started telling the media in India that he was willing to withdraw from the bid if the Glasgow-based company wasn't willing to reduce the price.

Mallya had done something similar with Sahara Airways which was up for sale. He had kept raising the offer price for the airline which led rival Jet Airways to keep topping it until one day Mallya suddenly withdrew from the bid stating that the price was too high. That left Jet as the sole bidder, forcing them to buy Sahara in spite of almost everyone stating that Jet's offer was too high for its own good. It proved to be true much later and it took Naresh Goyal's Jet several years to shrug off the losses from the deal.

On another occasion, United Spirits withdrew from another bid, this time, for the French company Champagne Taittinger, after the owners did not respond favourably.

After several rounds of negotiations, Imerman agreed to sell Whyte & Mackay but at a price which was much more than the company was worth.

On 16 May 2007, both Imerman and Mallya came

together on stage at Glasgow to announce that they had inked a deal. Mallya was to buy Whyte & Mackay for £595 million (about $1.2 billion). Mallya later told newspersons that he had an emotional connect with Whyte & Mackay as his father's favourite drink had been the Isle of Jura.

Whyte & Mackay had an inventory of 155 million litres of Scotch which was valued at between £350 million and £400 million. Its brands such as Dalmore Single Highland Malt and Vladivar Vodka were, at that time, valued at about £180 million.

But the price included £175 million of the company's debt. ICICI Bank and Citiground, Inc. handled the entire transaction.

What also came along with the company was the Invergordon distillery with a 40 million litre capacity per year, four malt distilleries in Scotland and a bottling plant in Grangemouth with a capacity of 12 million cases per year. The company also had a 3 per cent market share of the UK whisky market.

The SWA chief who was against the sale of Whyte & Mackay to Mallya, now realized that he had proved his point. Asked to comment, Hewitt said that it just showed how popular Scotch was and that it was important to sell only genuine Scotch. What he left unsaid was: 'See, you have just proved my point. Therefore stop producing illegal whisky and start importing the real Scotch at much lower tariffs.'

Still, it took the Indian government about five more years to bring down the taxes to some acceptable level. Acceptable to the European Union members.

Meanwhile, Mallya had borrowed heavily—as much as £325 million—against Whyte & Mackay's assets to fund the £595-million acquisition. But by 2012, the loss-making company had been turned around and was posting pre-tax profits.

Whyte & Mackay is again up for grabs as its new owner, Diageo, has been forced to sell the company so that it does not fall foul of UK's anti-trust law.

10

The Diageo Deal

Vijay Mallya was exiting the elevator to his penthouse on the top floor of his UB City headquarters, which looks like a miniature version of the Empire State Building, when he received a call from one of his old friends who was part of an advisory body appointed by Diageo, a British-owned liquor company.

During the short conversation, Mallya smiled often. The smile became broader as he made his way to his room and sat down. Once the call was over, he made several other calls, shot off some quick instructions to his staff and returned to the elevator.

Within hours, he was back in his private jet flying down to London. Mallya's friend was a well-known figure in the corporate circles in India. He also happened to be the chairman of one of the leading banks in the country and was sometimes referred to as the 'adviser to the country', often heading some of the key committees set up by the government. Various committees headed by him had a hand in advising various governments in the country on matters ranging from how to formulate the power tariff structure to rewriting the complex securities' market regulations.

Mallya's friend along with a few others was part of an advisory council recently set up by Diageo to monitor its Indian operations as well as grow its businesses there.

It hasn't been an easy journey for Diageo in India. It first set up its operations in the country sometime in 1994 as UDV India. But within a decade the London-based company exited India (in 2002) after selling its entire business which included Gilbey's Green Label. It must have been a combination of wrong advice and lack of vision which dictated Diageo's decision to withdraw from a market where its Green Label whisky had the third largest sales.

Realizing the folly of ignoring a country which was one of the fastest growing liquor markets in the world, Diageo came back through a joint venture with Radico Khaitan by launching Masterstroke whisky in 2006 and even roped in one of the Hindi film stars to promote the brand. Masterstroke never managed to fly off the shelves and the joint venture, Diageo Radico Distilleries, went kaput after six years.

Diageo later bought Seagram's brands in South Korea but declined to bid for the company's brands in India. It's competitor, Pernod Ricard, however, picked up Seagram's brands in India which included Blender's Pride, Royal Stag and Imperial Blue. Pernod Ricard went on to even eclipse the strongly entrenched United Spirits a decade later. For 2011–12, its net profit from its Indian operations was Rs 593 crore while that of United Spirits was Rs 343 crore.

There was more trouble in store for Diageo. In 2009, several of its executives and key officials, including its MD based out of India, Asif Adil, left the company suddenly. This apparently was the fallout of an internal investigation over an alleged misappropriation of funds, inventory mismanagement and inflated promotional expenses. Diageo, however, claimed that the exodus as well as subsequent reshuffle was part of an internal restructuring exercise.

In 2011, matters had come to a head. Following a

US-based stock exchange regulator Securities and Exchange Commission (SEC) investigation, Diageo agreed to pay $16 million, including a fine, after it was found guilty of corruption in India, South Korea and Thailand. The probe revealed that it had made illegal payments of over $2.7 million to government officials in violation of the US Foreign Corrupt Practices Act (FCPA), allegedly through its subsidiaries in these three countries so as to obtain sales and tax benefits for its Johnnie Walker and Windsor Scotch whiskies, among other brands.

In India, especially, from 2003 to mid-2009, illegal payments of over $1.7 million were allegedly made to hundreds of Indian government officials who were responsible for purchasing or authorizing the sale of Diageo's beverages in the country. Diageo earned more than $11 million in profits because of the increased sales resulting from these payments.

The SEC on its website said Diageo agreed to pay more than $16 million to settle the SEC's charges, apart from agreeing to cease and desist from further FCPA violations.

'For years, Diageo's subsidiaries made hundreds of illicit payments to foreign government officials,' said Scott W. Friestad, associate director of the SEC's

Division of Enforcement, in a statement. 'As a result of Diageo's lax oversight and deficient controls, the subsidiaries routinely used third parties, inflated invoices, and other deceptive devices to disguise the true nature of the payments.'

But all that was in the past. Diageo realized that if it had to immediately get down to business in India, then the only player it could hope to do so with was United Spirits. But valuations were proving to be a contentious issue. Mallya was on a stronger wicket. Talks between the two giants continued unhindered but would reach a dead end when it came to valuations. But by late 2009, it was becoming clear to Diageo that it was getting nowhere with its talks with Vijay Mallya for acquiring a stake in his United Spirits. 'Mallya is playing a game of poker here,' one of the key officials involved in the talks with United Spirits is believed to have remarked. Mallya, as they say, held all the aces.

But Diageo wouldn't let off the pressure. Its top executives kept visiting Bangalore to meet their counterparts in United Spirits. It set up a high-powered advisory council in 2011 to make it known to everyone its seriousness in expanding its operations in India. The council included Deepak

Parekh, the chairman of HDFC Bank; M.A. Alagappan, former executive chairman of the Murugappa Group; Ashok Ganguly, former chairman of Hindustan Unilever; Ravi Rajgopal, former MD of Diageo India; and Naresh Chandra, former Cabinet secretary in the Indian government.

A year later, the talks were taking some shape. It was a good enough development for Diageo to confirm to the shareholders as well as the media that it was in serious talks with United Spirits. But Mallya was more cautious. He told the media that while talks were on, they might not eventually lead to anything tangible.

But 55-year-old Paul Walsh, CEO of Diageo, was more than confident that the talks would eventually bear fruit. Known among his peers for his competitive spirit, he was credited with turning around Diageo into a global powerhouse, Walsh was initially criticized for knocking off several food brands from the Diageo shelves to focus fully on premium drinks. But that strategic decision had paid off in the long run.

Diageo, born from the merger of Grand Metropolitan, a property and brewing company, and Guinness, a drinks major, started as a major consumer goods company until Walsh stepped in as its CEO. He quickly realized that to compete with the likes of Unilever and other food giants, the company needed to pour enormous amounts of money and grow both organically as well as through acquisitions.

Hence, Diageo went about disposing of companies such as Pilsbury and Burger King to focus fully on growing the drinks business.

The next frontier to be conquered was India, though the decision to do so came much later and rather closer to Walsh's eventual exit from his CEO's job. The market was rather attractive: India's total liquor sale by volume was about 260 million cases per annum and growing in double digits. Within a decade it had become the third largest liquor market in the world and in value terms it was about $35 billion per annum. It was also the largest market for whisky in the world with six of the seven top selling brands in the world being Indian.

Apart from that, the Indian government's decision to reduce tariffs on imported liquor in a phased manner was intoxicating news for the British company. Hence, there were more opportunities than ever. Diageo had the money power to buy even some of the biggest brands in the world. With United Spirits in its kitty, Diageo would straight away have a market share of 45 per cent in India.

That crucial phone call to Mallya by one of the members of the advisory committee of Diageo was to inform him that the talks had reached a final stage and to ask him if he could fly down to London along with his officials for one last meeting before the deal was finalized.

In fact, in the last week of August 2012, a crucial management committee meeting among Diageo top executives in Singapore had been cut short as they had been called back to London to initiate a series of meetings with their counterparts in United Spirits. The then CFO and joint president of United Spirits, P.A. Murali, too, had rushed to London for the meeting.

When the talks between the two companies resumed in 2012, Kingfisher Airlines' net debt was $1.7 billion while the holding company of the group, UB Holdings, had pledged most of its shares to raise the funds from the bank for running the airline's operations. The situation for the UB Group couldn't have been worse.

It was a much wiser and poorer Mallya who

arrived in London for the talks. But Diageo knew that the acquisition would come at a high cost because of the huge share United Spirits commanded in the Indian market. The negotiations started in mid-2012 and Diageo was quick to realize that it was winning most of the rounds. The deal was finally struck on 9 November 2012; both companies announced in a joint statement that Diageo would buy a majority stake in United Spirits for $2.1 billion. Diageo would eventually end up with a stake of 53.4 per cent in the Indian company through a series of step-by-step acquisitions.

As per the deal, Diageo would get 27.4 per cent stake in the company from the promoters at a price of Rs 1440 per share and would then opt for an open offer to buy another 26 per cent at Rs 1400 per share from the rest of the shareholders. The entire transaction would result in United Spirits' stake being reduced to about 14.9 per cent.

At the press conference to announce the deal, Mallya made some brave statements stating that he was not selling his family jewel but was only embellishing it. He also defended the move to sell a majority stake in the company, stating that he had the shareholders' interest uppermost in his mind while taking a decision to sell a significant stake in United Spirits. He couldn't have put it better. After all, he was a shareholder too, holding a majority stake in his group companies.

Diageo's chief operating officer, Ivan Menezes, who took over from Walsh as the CEO, was from India. An alumnus of the prestigious Indian Institute of Management at Ahmedabad, Menezes had a very good track record in the company. A soft-spoken person, Menezes had been involved with the negotiations with the UB Group for several years. Once the deal went through, Menezes was rewarded for his efforts and promoted as the CEO.

Though the deal was signed, there was some trouble ahead for Diageo. It wasn't that easy for it to take control of the company it had wooed for several years.

The Indian antitrust regulator, the Competition Commission of India (CCI), raised objections to the deal, stating that it found certain clauses based on probabilities and not definitive in nature. The issue was about whether Diageo's entry would give the company an unfair advantage in the market as per section 20(4) of the Competition Act.

Earlier, the stock exchange regulator, SEBI too

had expressed reservations about the preferential allotment of shares to the acquirers if the open offer failed to get a good response from the non-promoter shareholders. It felt that minority shareholders might be at a disadvantage under the existing terms of the deal. SEBI, however, cleared the open offer after certain changes were carried out.

The CCI later cleared the deal, stating that it would boost the liquor brand market in India. It said that since Diageo and United Spirits operated in entirely different markets with different price points, there would be negligible overlaps between their products in each of the branded spirits segments.

However, in an analyst call, Gilbert Ghostine, president for Asia-Pacific for Diageo, did admit that the company was looking at exiting mass-end brands which did not make money. But 75 per cent of the volumes for United Spirits come from mass brands. Diageo may not have immediately spelt out its strategy, but it increasingly looks certain that it wants to have a larger play in the value segment, something which its competitor Pernod Ricard had so successfully done.

Ghostine is also believed to have said that even

on the margin front, it won't be able to match that of Pernod Ricard and it would take much more time to get several issues right.

After both the CCI and SEBI cleared the path for Diageo to operate in the country, the British giant had still some more issues to contend with. The open offer ironically was one of them.

The open offer price was fixed at Rs 1440 which was 7.2 per cent higher than the closing price a day before the public announcement of the deal was made. But from then onwards the stocks kept moving up. Days before the open offer was expected to be floated on 10 April 2013, the stocks had moved up to Rs 1800. Everyone expected the open offer price to be revised but a report from independent directors of Diageo said that the price was 'fair' and did not need to be revised. This put paid to the hopes of shareholders who expected the price to be revised upwards.

Once the share price had touched nearly Rs 2000, it became clear that very few would subscribe to the open offer. JM Financials, which was managing the open offer, said in a filing to the stock exchanges after the open offer closed that Diageo had just managed to pick up less than 1 per cent of the total shares as the stocks were trading at Rs 2304, much higher than the offer price.

While Diageo officials put up a brave front stating that they had factored in various issues facing the UB Group including several court cases against it, they began to realize that it would be a long time before they would actually get full control of the company.

Diageo had however began the process of increasing its stake in United Spirits. By July 2013, it had managed to acquire 25.02 per cent after investing Rs 5235.85 crore including the 10 per cent it bought through preferential allotment of new shares of 10 per cent of an expanded equity. It has, so far, spent a little less than $1 billion out of the total of $2 billion it plans to invest in its Indian operations to take its stake to 53 per cent.

Diageo, currently, is increasingly getting dragged into one controversy after another, following the court battles United Spirits faces on one issue or the other. The consortium of banks which had lent money to Kingfisher Airlines has filed for a winding up petition against the holding company, UBHL. An article in the *Economist* earlier had said that bankers in India were foolish enough to lend money to an entity under the pretence that it was a going concern. Terming them as timid, it said that they had the power to bring Mallya's empire down but wouldn't do so because they were not in the habit of confronting India's tycoons.

A year before this, when lenders actually started asking their money back, it was put across to Mallya's officials as gently as possible, a treatment they normally do not accord to small investors whose debt does not exceed a couple of crores. Instead of calling Mallya to their offices, the officials of the lenders' consortium were actually sent to the headquarters of the UB Group to hold meetings there. But instead of meeting Mallya in person, they would be asked to meet his officials who would make presentation after presentation telling them that they had a business plan in place which would take them out of the woods.

After several knocks on the door, Mallya did make an appearance at one of the meetings which sent the officials of the banks into delirium. 'You know, Mallya was kind enough to meet us. He actually made a very good presentation and was very courteous with us,' an official with a bank, which has substantial exposure to Kingfisher Airlines, said.

'We have faith in Mallya's turnaround plan,' the banker said on being asked whether the UB Group chairman had come forward with any commitments. In 2012 when Mallya said during a post-AGM press conference that some foreign airlines were in talks with Kingfisher Airlines to pick up equity, it sent the stocks soaring. Some of the lender banks actually believed his statement. 'Let us give him some more time because he has said that a foreign airline is interested in Kingfisher,' a bank official said.

After facing severe criticism from the media as well as the government, lenders led by the State Bank of India finally started taking action against the UB Group. Initially they started invoking the guarantees and later took the group to court. They finally got an interim order from the Karnataka High Court restraining UB Holdings and its chairman, Vijay Mallya, from alienating or transferring assets.

Such decisive action led Diageo to admit in a statement released to the stock exchanges that its move to acquire a further 27.4 per cent stake within the stipulated deadline set by stock market regulator SEBI had run into trouble as some of the banks had refused to release the pledged shares. United Spirits later filed a petition in court to direct the banks to release the shares but it has not met with any success so far.

It is not just the national banks which are after the UB Group now. In November 2013, a French bank, BNP Paribas filed a winding up petition against UB Holdings claiming corporate guarantees for $26.63 million given by the holding company of the UB Group to cover Kingfisher Airlines' acquisition of three ATR 72-212A aircraft in 2006.

Walsh and Menezes might have swung the deal in favour of their company and some might say at a far lesser price than what was thought earlier, but it hasn't been easy since then. Did the company actually rush into a deal, enamoured by the success of Pernod Ricard? Would it have been better if Diageo had ventured out on its own just as Pernod Ricard had done? The jury is still out but spending over $2 billion won't be enough. It will have to keep investing in working capital and capex as well as keep a watch on regulatory requirements so that what happened in 2011 does not come back to haunt the company.

Diageo in the second innings is trying to be as cautious as possible. For example, it has pulled United Spirits out of Tamil Nadu as it believes that to directly operate out of that state could force it to make certain compromises which would go against SEC regulations. Hence, the company has sold off its distillery and brewery businesses to another entity and has entered into a franchise arrangement for bottling as well as marketing its products with the same company.

As far as Mallya is concerned, he still remains chairman of United Spirits and United Breweries, though most of the crucial decisions are taken by joint venture partners Diageo and Heineken respectively.

Acknowledgements

To say that it was challenging to write this book would be an understatement. The first to refuse to involve himself with this project was the very subject of this book, Vijay Mallya.

After leaving him several messages and mails, Mallya called me up in the dead of night (and it is quite normal for him to do so) one day to find out what the book was all about.

When I had finished giving him details about the project, he flatly refused to be interviewed for the book, claiming that he was writing his autobiography and that he had sent his executive assistant to several parts of the world, to talk to various people associated with him as well as his companies to gather information for his book. 'I have hundreds of hours of transcript with me and I am in talks with a journalist of international repute to put it together.

Therefore, don't you think it will be a conflict of interest for me to participate in your project?'

I replied that he could write his own book; mine would be from the perspective of a journalist. But my pitch didn't go down well with him. Mallya warned me that his executives would not speak to me if he did not give them permission. A close associate of Mallya who organized religious rituals for him and sort of doubled up as his astrologer, and claimed he was Mallya's childhood friend, tried to be helpful: 'Why don't you read the (coffee table) book brought out on the occasion of his fiftieth birthday and write a similar one? I will tell you it will be a bestseller.'

There were some who were more forthright in their refusal to speak to me stating that they feared for their lives, making me wonder whether they thought of him as a mafia boss.

Like all of us, Mallya has his share of friends and foes, and if one is a business magnate like him, the number is multiplied several times over. He has also cultivated a large number of decision-makers as well as those in the media over the years. Getting an impartial view about him from them was never an easy task.

Acknowledgements

But all was not lost. Some of his friends, former employees, business competitors, distributors of his products and government officials opened up and were just a call away whenever I wanted to dip into their vast pool of information about the industry as well as about the man.

If I were to sum up the man, I would say that he is quite a lonely individual and according to my 'deep throat', he neither has permanent enemies nor permanent friends. That more or less defines Mallya.

~

I must admit I was working against severe time constraints (I also hold a regular day job) while writing this book, which was offered to me by Penguin after the publishers happened to read about a feature on Mallya I had written for *The Hindu*.

Though the book carries the name of only one author, there are several people behind the effort and I would be committing an unpardonable sin if I didn't use this opportunity to mention the contributions of at least some of them.

I have always wondered what made my 'deep throat' share with me several incidents in Mallya's life and put his friendship with him on thin ice. But

Acknowledgements

I now realize he wanted to tell Mallya's story to the outside world as much as I wanted to. His contribution in putting together this book was immense and I will always be eternally thankful to him for this huge gesture on his part. His only request to me was that I should be as objective as possible while writing about Mallya and I have tried my best to stick to the promise I made to him.

There were others who were associated with Mallya either as business partners or as employees who shared with me their experiences. They prefer to remain anonymous. My grateful thanks to them for helping me put together this book.

Penguin's commissioning editor, Anish Chandy, was manna from heaven. Without his constant encouragement and gentle goading, this book would not have seen the light of day. My heartfelt thanks to him for being such a wonderful human being. K.S. Dakshina Murthy, the online editor of Al Jazeera as well as editorial consultant for *The Hindu*, was the sheet anchor I leaned on heavily while writing the book. Being an author himself, his valuable tips came in extremely handy and I am ever grateful to him for being very supportive while I was writing the book.

Ganapathi Mudur, the science editor of the *Telegraph*,

helped me put together the outline for the book which was approved by the publishers immediately. I can't thank him enough for his gesture.

I will fail in my duty if I don't thank my former editor and director of Kasturi & Sons, K. Venugopal, who has been a constant source of encouragement.

Former editor of *The Hindu Business Line*, D. Sampath Kumar readily gave his approval on behalf of the newspaper when I informed him about the offer from Penguin. My sincere thanks to him for making it easier for me to write my first book. I would also like to thank my colleagues, N. Ramakrishnan and Raghuvir Srinivasan, who have been of great support while I was writing the book.

My friends Krishnaprasad, B.B. Subhash, R. Rajkamal and Vasuki Prasad and my brother, Guruprasad went through the manuscript and gave me valuable suggestions, all of which have been incorporated in the book.

My wife, Rashmi, and my son, Madhav, allowed me the kind of space only they could give while I spent long hours away from them, writing the book. Being a bibliophile herself, Rashmi's suggestions have been of invaluable help in making this book, hopefully, a better read. Their patience and affection will have a special place in my heart forever.